Home & Habitat

Selected Stories and Poems by Senior Writers
from Elkhart, Jasper and St. Joseph Counties
in Indiana and Holmes County, Ohio

GREENCROFT COMMUNITIES

Acknowledgements:
Back cover: "Sisters Scape" quilt, 94" by 82", pieced by Anne Raftree, resident of Greencroft Goshen, Goshen, Indiana. It portrays the landscape of central Oregon where Anne lived for over 35 years, with the Three Sisters mountains, ponderosa pines, mountain wildflowers and rivers of salmon. This quilt won First Place for Soft Crafts at the 2013 Art Is Ageless contest and exhibit for senior artists of Elkhart County, Indiana, sponsored by Greencroft Communities.

Library of Congress Control Number: 2013952066

ISBN: 978-1-4675-9065-5

Printed in the United States of America by Mennonite Press, Inc., Newton, KS 67114. www.MennonitePress.com

*Dedicated to seniors who share their gift of writing
to inspire, enlighten and entertain people of all ages.*

Contents

Introduction vii

Foreword ix

Stories

Loretta Vandiver Rea *In a Little Red Barn on a Farm
Down in Indiana* 1
Excellence in Writing Award

Edith L. Allen *A Visit to Grandpa and Grandma's 1940* 4

John M. Bender *Katie and Rachel Save the Day* 6

Mabel V. Brunk *The Legacy of Cousins* 9

Martha A. Burger *The Kitchen Table* 11

Pat Clark *Lives Enriched Through Hand-Me-Downs* 13

Carlyle Frederich *Poor and Don't Know It* 16

Annabelle Herschberger *The Blizzard of 1978* 18

Ruby E. Hershberger *When We Became Electrified* 20

Karen Y. Hoover *Snapshots of a Farm Life* 22

Marian E. Hostetler *The Store* 25

Mary Kauffman *Children Are a Heritage* 27

Steve Kruse *Got Knob Grass?* 30

Roberta Carpenter Leonard *Awakening of a Cold
Winter Morning* 32

Roberta Carpenter Leonard *Innocence in the
Midst of Turmoil* 34

Roberta Carpenter Leonard *Learning to Live in a
Dilapidated House* 36

RoseMary McDaniel *A Tribute Letter to My Grandfather* 38

Alvin Miller *The Surprise Blizzard* 40

B.J. Miller *A Sod House on the Prairie* 42

Stephen J. Miller *The Dog Biscuits of Life* 44

Millie Myers *My Dad* 45

Carol Parker *Our Farmhouse: Every Animal's Habitat* 47

Leslie Reid *Mystery in the Meadow* 49
Wes Richard *Life's Boundaries* 51
Bonnie L. Smith *I Was Young Once* 54
Bonnie L. Smith *The Little House Down the Lane* 56
Arleta Unzicker *Scenes of My Childhood* 58

Poetry

Roberta Carpenter Leonard *The Drought* 63
   Excellence in Writing Award
Wanda A. Alwine *I Ain't Dead Yet* 64
John M. Bender *January 1969* 66
Martha A. Burger *Mom's Birthday* 67
Jim Carpenter *It's Late Afternoon* 69
Jim Carpenter *The May Garden* 70
Lois T. Clark *The Winter of Our Discontent* 72
Annabelle Herschberger *The Change of Seasons* 73
Roberta Carpenter Leonard *Mama's Washday* 74
Roberta Carpenter Leonard *Salute to Volunteer Firemen* 75
Roberta Carpenter Leonard *The Warring Sky* 77
Richard E. Martin *A Vision of Beauty on a Gray Day* 78
Alta Roth Mellinger *Cross Cultural Crafts* 79
Margaret J. Metzler *Christmas 1979* 80
Margaret J. Metzler *Look Them in the Eye* 83
Henri Lee Richards, Sr. *Native American* 84
Daniel Roll *The Diary* 85
Bill Sheldon *Boat Mates* 86
Erma N. Yoder *December Questions* 88
Erma N. Yoder *STUFF* 89

Contest Sponsor

Greencroft Communities 90

Introduction

Comedy and tragedy are two different ends of the dramatic spectrum. Over the course of a lifetime we experience much of both of these. The prose and poetry in this book will bring such stories to you through the written voices of people who have lived long, interesting lives. These writers have faced many of life's challenges and have persevered. Some of the stories will make you chuckle, others may bring tears to your eyes. Perhaps you will see your own or your family's experiences in these stories. I am most grateful for these stories, and for the authors who have written from their hearts. It is so interesting to see what "home" has been and meant from a variety of perspectives.

I hope these writings also inspire you to write *your* stories. You have many experiences and insights to share with others — your own family, your friends, others whom you have not even met. Just the very act of writing will be good for your brain, if not your soul. Write, and share your writing. You too have something from which the rest of us can learn.

And encourage the older people in your life to share their stories. Perhaps they can write them up, perhaps you can assist. These days it is also easier to record people telling their stories, to preserve them in their own voice or to later put them in print.

Living life in one's encore years means allowing God to creatively use us, just as we have allowed God to do when were were younger and engaged in professional and "home" careers. Today God uses all of creation to draw that creation closer to God. At all times in life allow God to use the creativity given to you to tell of God's wonder and might in our world and in our "home."

We all have experienced "Home" in a variety of ways and places. Tell the stories!

Mark King
President and Chief Executive Office
Greencroft Communities

Foreword

Story. The longer I work in communication the more convinced I become that story telling is the strongest way to convey a message. Stories draw us in. They give us information, emotion, truth and non-truth in ways that enable us to experience things from the other's point of view. Story teaches, story builds empathy, story draws us together, story enraptures us.

Stories have several components. One is the text of the story, the message in the words and images. Another aspect is the way it is written — the delivery if you will — the style, phrasing and rhythm that transports us in an extra special way. I believe you will find a wonderful mix of these components in the pieces in this book.

There are stories here with humor and stories with sadness. Stories about wonderful events and stories about very hard times. Some of the writing is pleasant, some of it quite deep. There are some events and themes that recur throughout the book: the Great Depression, World War II, Christmas, seasons. And of course change, an ever-present part of life. And much, much thanks too for family, friends and faith.

The stories in this book are entries from a 2013 contest held by Greencroft Communities to celebrate the creativity and life experiences of senior adults through their writing. Greencroft Communities is a regional retirement organization, providing a continuum of care from independent living and at-home services to assisted living and skilled nursing care at six communities in Indiana and Ohio serving some 2,000 residents.

Greencroft Communities regularly holds creative contests for older adults. There was a previous book in 2008, *Crossing the Frontier*. There were music contests in 2006 and 2010, which resulted in compact discs of the winners' performances, *Singing Through the Generations* and *Seniors To Note*. And 2014 will be the 10th year for our annual Art Is Ageless contest and exhibit for senior artists in a variety of artistic media—drawing, painting, photography, quilting, needlework, ceramics, sculpture, woodworking and more. Each year a calendar is created showcasing the beautiful winning art pieces from the contest.

There are conditions and guidelines for these events. For the contest that has resulted in this book, the writers must have lived in a county where there is one of the affiliate communities of Greencroft Communities. These are Elkhart, Jasper and St. Joseph Counties in Indiana and Holmes County in Ohio. The writers must have been at least 55 years old. And there were maximum lengths for the essays and poems.

The contest that resulted in this book was given the theme "Home and Habitat." Writers were instructed to write about "growing up in their particular location and life. Any place and any time of life is appropriate — from childhood through teenage years to raising a family through retirement, at home or at work, with family or on one's own, a rural setting or the big city or another country. Each person and each place is distinctive and provides insights into life."

Over 50 authors submitted some 100 entries to the contest. They were evaluated for the strength of the topic, the quality of writing, the unique "voice" that the piece conveyed and the connection to the "Home and Habitat" theme.

This book does not contain every entry. There were entries from places outside the eligible areas (counties where there is a Greencroft Communities facility). There were entries that were too long (several of which could nearly be a book by themselves!). Some entries did not strongly connect to the theme. And still there were too many, so some hard choices had to be made in order to keep the book to the intended size. Some writers did not have their entry chosen and several writers have more than one work in the book.

One piece among the submissions for both stories and poems was chosen for an "Excellence Award." That work is first in each category. The pieces that follow are alphabetical by author.

I take responsibility for any errors that appear in the book. If you find one I trust that it will not stop you from continuing to read and appreciate the writer's storytelling. "Thank you"s to Greencroft Communities' Jennifer Hayes, Vice President of Marketing and

Corporate Development, and Mark King, President and CEO, for their support of our creativity contests for older adults.

We gratefully thank the many writers who submitted so many wonderful pieces. Creativity certainly does not end as life progresses! It has been truly gratifying and inspiring to work with the entries. I am in awe of the storytelling gifts that this book represents. I hope that in reading these stories and poems that you too will be reminded of the importance of "home" and can find its blessing in your own experiences and memories.

Jon Kauffmann-Kennel
Home and Habitat Editor
Director of Media & Public Relations, Greencroft Communities

Stories

Loretta Vandiver Rea
Bremen, Indiana
Excellence in Writing—Essay

In a Little Red Barn on a Farm Down in Indiana

A song by this same title, written in 1934, was the theme song for the WOWO morning radio program hosted by Bob Sievers out of Ft. Wayne, Indiana. I lived with my parents and sister on the family farm where we had a red barn, but at that time the song didn't mean a thing to me.

While driving the tractor for my Dad I had often imagined a little red barn-shaped house built near the trees, even though at that time I didn't plan to live there. I remember that scorching August day when I was cleaning out the barn and wrestling huge flies, bussing around my head, all while trying to hold my breath from the wet straw stench. I decided farm living was not the life for me, and then a reverse concept of the popular television show "Green Acres" became my dream.

When I married, it was to a city boy, and for the next 30-plus years his job had us setting up residence in places I had never even imagine visiting. Our daughter had just turned three years old and our son was almost two when we moved to Pago Pago, American Samoa and lived on an 18-mile long island in the South Pacific between Hawaii and New Zealand. After a couple of years in the tropical rain forest living with tree-ripened bananas, orchids, fresh pineapple, white sand and the constant rhythm of the waves, we moved to the desert.

Artesia, New Mexico reminds me of a Western movie set. That thought came to me the day I first saw a tumbleweed dance in the breeze, down Main Street, dodging the oil rigging. We visited Carlsbad Caverns several times, enjoyed the local folklore, gathered "Pecos Diamonds" and witnessed fluffy white cotton maturing in the fields. Pecos Diamonds are unusual, small quartz crystals that vary in color from transparent to translucent white, red, yellow and some nearly black. We fell in love with the friendly people, the mild winter climate and the overall charm of the Southwest, including the sign of businessmen wearing cowboy hats and boots with their suits.

My husband's work took us to New England, halfway between Boston and New York City. We enjoyed day trips as well as accompanying visiting family and friends to sightsee, attend Broadway shows and to shop. We saw the Rockettes perform at Radio City Music Hall, rode horse-drawn carriages in Central Park and often visited the Statue of Liberty. We lived in Connecticut and I was definitely off "Green Acres."

As time passed I longed to return to Indiana to live, although at least once a year (some years twice and one year three times) we traveled the 821 miles by plane, Amtrak train, minivan or VW bug. Yes, you read that correctly, Volkswagen Beetle. It was a time when the only car available was our VW Bug. Our two children plus the dog occupied the back seat; we mailed our luggage ahead, packed the trunk like a suitcase with several days' worth of clothing and then took three days driving each way.

The trips back to Connecticut after visiting in Indiana went from difficult to painful. I once broke down and cried after seeing an Indiana license plate on the car in front of me in line in Connecticut. We began to think about retirement and moving back to Indiana.

One morning in May of 2007 I woke up feeling 30 years older than my 57 years. The diagnosis was Parkinson's disease; it had hit hard and fast. My husband's employer was agreeable to having him work remotely from home and that could be from Indiana.

We sold the house in Connecticut, moved and built the red house in the shape of a barn on the family farm near that cluster of trees in the field. Its location is the spot my eyes would find as a young girl while gazing out my bedroom window, wondering what was ahead for me. Our house is unique, accessible, casual, comfortable and convenient. It is decorated throughout in a barn theme, including life-size ceramic roosters, denim-upholstered living room furniture, barrels, buckets, wire egg baskets, tractor seats, milk cans and so on.

We call our portion of the family farm Rise Early Acres, because the first letter of each word spells out our last name Rea.

I'm back where I began, I'm older and wiser and I love living in a little red barn on a farm down in Indiana.

Excellence in Writing—Essay
Loretta writes about the young person's desire to get away from the overly familiar and mundane. She gives vivid descriptions of making "home" in a variety of wonderful, sometimes exotic, locations. Yet there is an inner urge, or tug to find peace of mind that often leads us back "home," to a psychological and spiritual, if not physical, place. This is a fulfilling circle that life's journey often provides.

Edith L. Allen
New Carlisle, Indiana

A Visit to Grandpa and Grandma's 1940

In 1940 I was five years old and lived on a dairy farm in Flushing, Michigan with my family — Dad, Mom, two brothers, George (older by five years) and Erwin (who was born that June) and our hired man Orville.

Once a month our family drove to Grandpa (Walter Clayton) and Grandma (Sarah Elizabeth Stafford) Hier's in Chapin for Sunday dinner. I loved going there, as Aunt Zelda, Uncle Griff and cousins Wanda and Dale would also come there from Lansing. (I am 10 days older than Dale and had to remind him every visit. Come to think of it, I still do.) They always brought hot dogs and buns, bologna and soft store-bought bread, cheese — oh, wonderful cheese — and last but not least, store-bought cookies for dinner. What a treat. I have never gotten over my admiration for those two meats. Of course, now the home-canned beef, pork and chicken that we had to eat all the time would taste mighty good.

Grandpa and Grandma's house in town (Chapin had about half a dozen houses and a store) had a hand-painted sign in front that said "Saws-Knives Sharpened." There was a stone wheel with a seat and paddles he used to sharpen tools and knives. Dale and I could really get the wheel moving.

Grandpa Hier chewed tobacco. In the living room there was a big stove that stood between Grandpa and Grandma's rocking chairs. Grandpa's chair was on the left so he could open that stove door and spit. We never did figure out how he did that without missing the stove opening. It probably sounds a bit disgusting now, but as a kid it was fascinating to watch Grandpa. And, of course, laughing when Grandma got after him for doing that. There was always room on his lap for Dale and me to sit and rock.

On the buffet was a beautiful pink-covered jar that Grandpa

always kept filled with gingersnaps. In their living room was a piece of furniture that the top opened up and little round discs fit on, a needle lowered down, you cranked the handle and music, beautiful music, came out. George and Wanda, being 10 years old, were the ones allowed to operate this machine. Oh would I like to have that piece of furniture today.

Grandma Hier always wore dresses a couple of inches above her ankles, always wore a wrap-around apron, always was ready with a soft, snuggly hug and smelled of Fels-Naptha soap. Life certainly wasn't easy for her but she never complained and we kids never knew. She never had inside water, always cooked on a wood stove, had no refrigerator, fresh meat (mostly pork) was cooked and packed under lard in crocks in the basement, which had an outside "cellar door." They didn't call it a basement; it was a "root cellar" where vegetables and fruit were kept. During the summer months if they needed ice for the ice box, a card was put in the window to let the iceman know to stop.

While the adults visited my cousins, brother and I ran around at loose ends, inventing games, wandering their property, climbing trees and playing at the creek. We had to leave for home by 4:00 because Dad had to get home to do the milking. Somehow, when the weather was warm, I always went home with wet feet because my cousin Dale and I always managed to fall into the creek.

John M. Bender
Elkhart, Indiana

Katie and Rachel Save the Day

April 3, 1950. We set off for school. I, in first grade, walked; Sanford, in third grade, biked. I cut through our woods, the spring wildflowers making a run for it before the leaves on the maple, beech, elm and oak trees would block out much of the sunlight. Robins flitted in the school yard.

We lived two miles east and south of our one-room public school, located in East Zorra Township of dairy-rich Oxford County, Province of Ontario, Canada. My paternal grandparents, Solomon and Rachel Bender, lived a hop, skip and jump from our farm. My maternal grandparents, Christian and Catherine (Katie) Bender (yes, Mom was a Bender too), lived on a farm two miles west and south of school.

My parents, Lloyd and Leona, were married on New Year's Day 1939 at Mom's home. For five years they lived in the extended household that included Annie Kennel Bender (granddad's mother), Chris and Katie, and Mom's three younger brothers. Sanford and I became the fourth generation living under one roof.

In spring 1944 we moved in with Solomon and Rachel until the house on the farm my parents had purchased was vacated. Willard was born during our stay with Solomon and Rachel. Three more siblings were born on the farm where we grew up.

Out of the blue, that afternoon while at school, the sky opened and cascaded down like Niagara Falls. The cloudburst washed out the road halfway home. Word came to the school that neighbors would help children across the impassible gully. At the same time one of our neighbors sent word to the teacher that I was to go to my grandparent's home. Which grandparents? Sanford and a classmate already must have raced off toward home. In my seven-year-old's reckoning, the message meant I should change course, since I often stopped in at Rachel and Solomon's anyway, and go west to Chris and

Katie's home. I rode with four of the Schumm children in the pony cart they sometimes drove to school. At the 16th Line they turned north, I walked south.

Grandmother Katie was surprised to see me. I told her, tears almost welling, what I had been told. Surprisingly, Katie made little of my mistake; in fact, she welcomed me with open arms. She embraced me with keenest delight. She called Grandma Rachel. My parents had to take one of the children to the doctor in New Hamburg, Rachel said, and I was to have stopped with her. Grandma Katie told her that Granddad, who wasn't yet home, would bring me home after supper.

The memories of how Katie and Rachel seamlessly, consolingly, lovingly saved the day, and Rachel another day two months later, remain my priceless possessions.

On Thursday, June 8, on my walk home from school, Grandma Rachel met me at the end of their short driveway. I should stay with her, she said, since Dad and Mom had gone to be with Granddad Chris; Grandma Katie had taken ill during the night. She had died. Died? I was dumbfounded. It couldn't be. I sat in the hedge along the road and sobbed. Grandma Rachel did what she could to console me. Grandma Katie had died of a stroke, a month shy of her 59th birthday. (Five months earlier, great-grandmother Annie (Mem) had died, age 85.)

The *Tavistock Gazette* reported, "Mrs. Bender rested at the Robert Krug Funeral Home, Tavistock, until five o'clock Friday afternoon, when the remains were moved to her late resident, lot 28, con. 15, and where a service was held Sunday afternoon at two o'clock, followed by a memorial service at the East Zorra Amish Mennonite Church, 16th Line, and burial in the adjoining cemetery…. Upwards of 1,000 attended the church service, during which the Nightingale Chorus of Kitchener… sang." Mom's brothers, Orie, Harold and Ross, sang in the chorus.

From as far away as Michigan, Ohio, Indiana and New Mexico, came friends and relatives, drawn together to say goodbye. Many returned to Grandmother's late residence to visit and share the evening meal. Uncharacteristically, or maybe not, to us children the gathering seemed more like a reunion than a somber farewell.

More than 60 years on, lessons my grandmothers taught me still hit home: While storms can devastate, the sun will shine again; mistakes are not only OK, they often have a silver lining; like the Spring Beauty, we flourish for a season; kindness to a child lasts a lifetime; God comforts those who mourn; love endures; life flows on. Grandmothers save the day.

John was the editor of Crossing the Frontier, *the previous book of senior writings published by Greencroft Communities*

Mabel V. Brunk
Goshen, Indiana

The Legacy of Cousins

"You have 51 first cousins?" My friend could count her first cousins on one hand. What a deprived childhood she must have had. My sisters and brothers and I had grown up thinking everyone had lots of cousins. Our holidays were extra-special when shared with relatives. I remember one cold Thanksgiving day when my older brother and his same-age cousin poured water on our driveway, trying to create a frozen surface for skating or hockey. I was overjoyed one Christmas to find a new cousin had arrived at Aunt Amanda's home. Tired of always being my family's youngest child, I offered my entire savings (a new dollar bill and a shiny penny) to my aunt in exchange for their baby. But at least I was no longer the youngest cousin.

Living in a small town, we children treasured visits to cousins living on farms. At our aunt's home we climbed the big trees and instigated fights with water or over-ripe tomatoes. We walked barefoot along the dusty road, picking trumpet vine flowers to adorn our fingers. At our uncle's dairy farm we watched older cousins milking cows. Expert hands pinged the stream of milk against the bucket as the foamy liquid rose higher. When the cows were in pasture, we younger cousins took turns being "cows," standing in the stanchions and chewing the food.

A highlight of visits to Virginia cousins was a trip to the beach. I remember the first smell of ocean air. We ran to play in the water. We buried each other in the sand and feasted on watermelons, with seed-spitting contests.

Other cousins lived in a Washington, D.C. row house. We marveled at these cousins' tiny front yard bordered by a metal fence and gate. The Good Humor truck came almost to their front door. Grown-up cousins sometimes visited us. Cousin Wilmer's visits meant standing in line for a ride in his car's rumble seat.

Our parents enjoyed their cousins. Driving across Ohio meant a stop at Mama's jolly cousins Kate and Phoebe and a visit to their flowery greenhouse. A trip to Virginia meant getting chunks of bulk sweet chocolate and freshly baked bread at Papa's cousin Cora's bakery. My mother's first cousins gathered annually for a "Jacob and Anna Yoder Family Reunion." The postcard announcing the date was the centerpiece of our family's summer calendar. Wayne, Allen, Start and Mahoning Counties in Ohio, Warwick County in Virginia and Elkhart County in Indiana were the sites of the annual reunions hosted by our mother's cousins. At these reunions before and after the noon meal we children joined assorted ages of cousins in play. Whether we were first, second or once-removed cousins didn't matter to us.

Ties with cousins continue to be important in my adult years. My mother's cousins no longer hold an annual reunion. But my first cousins have initiated triennial gatherings. We like to remember childhood pranks and stories about our parents and grandparents.

In today's world smaller families and their separation by geography make "prospects for future cousinly gatherings a bit dim." I echo these words and other words of Johanna Garfield: "I feel lucky to be in what may be the last American generation to be the luxury of picking and choosing among a large number of semi-siblings (cousins)—separate enough to have an exotic appeal, yet bound to us through powerful ties of heredity and heritage."* I treasure memories from a childhood enriched by my cousins, who in our adult years continue to add spice to my life.

* *Johanna Garfield, "How Cousins Enrich Our Lives" (originally in* Ms., *Dec. 1984 and condensed in* Reader's Digest, *Apr. 1987)*

Martha A. Burger
Goshen, Indiana

The Kitchen Table

The old wooden kitchen table in the house where I lived, from the time I was nearly four years old until I left at nearly 18 to become a nurse, is about eight feet long and four feet wide. It is still in use. I don't know who made it or where it came from but it probably came with us when we moved to the house on my grandfather's farm in the winter of 1938.

Mostly it was used as a dining table but it has seen many other uses and has been moved from the back room, the original kitchen, to the dining room that is now the kitchen. When it is pulled away from the wall to make room for more people to sit around it, the legs always have to be straightened.

The surface is scrubbed smooth of any finish and is slightly bowed. Mama kept it covered with what she called "oilcloth." On butchering day the cover was removed and the table was used as a cutting surface for the chunks of fat being prepared for rendering lard.

Mama could spread out her ironing pad on the table. She never did have an ironing board. I never did quite get the hang of flattening out a starched white shirt to get all the wrinkles ironed out the way that she did.

While I was at home there was no sink in the kitchen, so after meals the round aluminum dishpan and the enamel drying tray were placed on the table. Water was carried from the cold water spring in back of the house and heated on the wood stove to wash the dishes using homemade lye soap. After the dishes were washed and dried the pans were hung on the wall behind the stove.

A couple of times a week Mama baked bread. Then the big blue crock was brought to the table where she mixed and kneaded the dough. While the over was heated for baking break she also made cookies and pies and rolled out the dough on the tabletop.

The kitchen table was covered with jars, can lids and sealing rings on canning days, as well as the peaches, pears, beans, corn, cherries, peas or grapes that were being preserved for later use, depending on the season. She also made huckleberry, strawberry and peach jam.

Once a year when the threshing crew came, the table was surrounded by hungry men. Sometimes it took two sittings to feed all of them. The women and girls ate later.

At spring cleaning time when the walls and ceiling were washed down, standing on the kitchen table made it easier to reach the ceiling. My sister and I did that.

Mama sat at the kitchen table when she wrote letters, figured up her egg account or worked the daily crossword puzzle in the newspaper. She also spread out her sewing materials there and used her portable Singer sewing machine to make most of our clothing and household goods. My siblings and I did our homework there with our backs to the warmth of the stove.

My parents are no longer living and the kitchen is a bit more modern. Now there is a combination electric/wood-burning store, a refrigerator, central heat and a sink with running water. The table is still the centerpiece of the kitchen, but now it is covered with plastic instead of oilcloth. The feeling is still the same when I go back to visit my brother, who lives there now. We do our talking at the table, look at old pictures, have a cup of tea and remember when....

Pat Clark
Granger, Indiana

Lives Enriched Through Hand-Me-Downs

Events or heirlooms often earn the designation of "Family Traditions." They are the fabric that weaves the history of our ancestors. These threads become time-honored collections, evoking memories from the past while dusting them off and revisiting each with the next generation.

Framed in my thoughts is a childhood tradition that brings back the sense of joy we felt every year in our home. It was the magic of seeing Christmas come to life. This was a special gift our parents gave to their eight children, year after year, as we celebrated the meaning of Christmas, and welcomed the holidays into our house.

While neighbors' homes glimmered with lights, the only hints of the approaching holiday at 1281 E. McKinley Street were cookies neatly stored in containers, unopened greeting cards and carols playing on the radio. We never had a Christmas tree until Christmas morning. Bedtime was after midnight mass on Christmas Eve as the clock approached 2 a.m.

At dawn, joy erupted in squeals of delight as we woke to discover Mom and Dad had worked through the night to transform our home into a winter wonderland. The view was enchanting. A magnificent tree glowing with lights and glass ornaments reflecting in the window panes graced our living room. The scent of fresh pine tingled our nostrils as daylight ushered in Christmas morning. Mom's handmade angels and a collection of decorations that each of us made in school hung at the front of our tree for everyone to admire. In the dining room, a blanket of snow covered the buffet where a manger rested on a pedestal, majestic with figurines of Mary, Joseph and baby Jesus.

Beginning Anew

In 1967, recently married, I hoped to start a holiday tradition with my husband John that would serve as our family's legacy. We could not afford a tree, lights or fancy ornaments. Instead, I gathered some pine boughs from our yard and tied red ribbons around them in an effort to create the holiday spirit. A friend gave us a small artificial tree the following year. I purchased a holiday magazine and worked feverishly to make ornaments to match the photos in the Christmas issue. I remember making my first angel reminiscent of those mother created years ago.

When people came to visit, we invited them to select an ornament from our tree as their gift. Once Christmas was over, there was little packing to do since most of the decorations now adorned trees of family and friends. For several years, I crafted the ornaments that became our gifts to everyone, making this our family tradition. Forty years later, those same decorations grace trees in homes we visit during the holidays. Seeing them gives us an opportunity to recollect fond memories tucked away from Christmas past.

A Third Generation

In December 2007 our daughter Diana and her husband Ryan adopted a young boy named Nathan. Shortly before the holidays Di asked her dad, now a grandpa, if he could remember conversations with Santa that she and her brother Robert had as youngsters. For years, a neighbor would call our home on Christmas Eve, pretending to be from the North Pole. Our children had taken great delight in those chats. Remembering their joy, Grandpa volunteered to phone our grandson and pretend to be Santa. We think Nate fell for it. The youngster asked Santa if he had a red nose like Rudolph's. Grandpa said Mrs. Claus was making him wear a scarf so his face didn't get cold while guiding his sleigh that night. Before hanging up, Nathan told Santa he would leave a cupcake and some "meeillk," as he likes to say, on the kitchen counter for him. Now our grandchild enjoys these calls and looks forward to them every year.

Links to the Future

Over time we started a new tradition that differs from years past. Our daughter's family prefers decorating their home after Thanksgiving dinner. As part of the festivities, we gift them with an ornament she selects from our tree that brings back memories of earlier celebrations. On Christmas morning we gather at her home to exchange gifts and enjoy brunch. Conversations tend to travel back in time as we reminisce about days gone by. We even have some of our earliest holiday conversations with our children preserved on audio tapes. As I look at my parents' buffet, now adorned with my nativity set, I realize traditions are the memories that give our family a unique identity. We move forward through life, while the spirit of the past links each generation together with treasures to be handed down to future generations.

Carlyle Frederick
Goshen, Indiana

Poor and Don't Know It

To be called rich or poor depends on the people to whom someone is being compared, such as a Mexican farmer or a New York lawyer. As a 12-year-old child in 1933, I really didn't know we were "poor." When I went from a rural one-room school to that "big" high school in Nappanee, I had not seen much of the world outside of my own home, church and neighborhood. We lived on a small 60-acre farm four miles from Foraker, Indiana. My dad was a free minister and a hard-working farmer. We had chickens, pigs, cows, horses, a large garden, lots of fruit trees that Dad had planted from seeds, and did our own butchering, curing and canning. My clothes were hand-me-downs outgrown by my brother or cousin, or made by my expert seamstress mother. Our income came from the sale of small amounts of milk, eggs, pigs and grain. We often took eggs to Weaver's store in Foraker and exchanged them for things we could not produce ourselves.

In addition to the general store, Foraker had a feed mill, a cider mill, a barbershop (15-cents), a blacksmith, Case tractor and implement sales, a lumber and coal supply, a bank, a post office and a big pickle factory. We grew two acres of pickles. I hated to pick them, but I loved taking them to the pickle factory and watching them put the pickles in large 10-foot vats and shovel salt from a train car into the vats.

I had saved a little money and had a small savings account in the Foraker bank. When it was closed in 1933, I lost a couple of dollars. But I must have ignored other people's money problems. I was not hungry. We had plenty to eat from our barn, chicken house, garden and orchard. The wood from our trees kept us warm (cutting and splitting it was hard work, however). Years later my older sister told me that we had almost lost the farm because our parents could not make the mortgage payments. A friend or relative had helped them out for awhile. I had not been aware of that.

I admit I was sometimes a bit envious of some friends who had things I did not have. But now I am glad I grew up during the Depression. I gained many value and habits that helped me face life's ups and downs. Our parents taught us to work hard to succeed, save what we could and not waste anything. I still have trouble throwing anything away. I keep thinking, "I might need it sometime."

I'm not poor. I guess I never was, really. I have a great family and friends, and a great place to live. After 39 years of employment and 29 years of retirement, I'm still a penny pincher. I believe my children and grandchildren think I'm "Rich and Don't Know It."

Annabelle Herschberger
Millersburg, Ohio

Finding Home in the Blizzard of 1978

It was on a Saturday of '78 and fluffy white flakes were doming down fast and furious! A large estate auction, located just east of Goshen, Indiana, was in session nearly all day. Interested buyers and collectors attended from miles away for this attraction. There were warnings of the impending storm, of which local people were aware and heeded the call to go home and stay.

It was close to evening hours when travelers far from home left, intending to go home, and were soon to be trapped, unaware of the hazards that lay ahead. Some of these people were heading north on State Road 13 for Michigan or intending to use the toll road just north of Middlebury for their Ohio and Illinois destinations. Traveling north only a short distance, the road was entirely impassible because of huge snow drifts. The stopping place was at the corner of State Road 13 and County Road 26, and the house on the corner looking inviting.

The occupants of the first stalled car walked up to the house, knocked, and discovered it to be unlocked and unoccupied. So they entered, turned on the lights and were soon ushering in many more stranded travelers. It so happened that the renters of the house were in the process of moving that day and couldn't come back for the last contents. The owners of the house were enjoying their winter stay in Florida and their son Perry was to look after the house.

Close neighbors walked over to check on the commotion, and soon came back with a big kettle of soup for the guests. A few of the travelers also had groceries in their cars that they brought in to share.

The neighbors contacted Perry, who was unable to get through, even though living only one-and-a-half miles away. It wasn't until late Sunday afternoon that the snowplow was able to open the road, and when Perry's family came to check the house they found everything

' notes all over the house describing
had getting acquainted with each
house to sleep, cooking and cleaning
riends.

Ruby E. Hershberger
Millersburg, Indiana

When We Became Electrified

It was the long hot summer of 1936. For two weeks, one in July and
one in August, daytime temperatures reached 100° Fahrenheit or
above. Gardens and lawns were brown and dry. Pastures were dry and
the livestock had a difficult time grazing.

We lived south of Middlebury, Indiana on State Road 13 near
what was then known as the Cable Line Road just one-half mile west.
Electric lines were on State Road 13 but did not branch off on the
gravel roads unless one paid the power company to install power to
the homes. The cost was high and so it didn't often happen. We were
without. Therefore we sweltered in the heat.

I was in a body cast from my waist on down, the result of right
hip surgery. It was hot and itchy under that cast. Very itchy. I had
shrunk a little but there was not enough room for my small hand
to go underneath the cast to scratch the itch. Oh, how I wished for
something to scratch. Enter my great-uncle Tobe, who raised turkeys.
He brought me a long white turkey feather which I could stick down
in the cast and scratch my belly. Talk about relief!

Mother had ways to make me more comfortable. She took our
bed pillows into the cool basement every morning and brought them
up each evening for us to enjoy a cool pillow to go to sleep. Another
treat was making lemonade. Slicking the lemons into thin slices, add
sugar, then squash until very juicy, add water and a few chips of ice
from our icebox. Delicious and refreshing!

In 1944 we got electricity. By then we lived on a dairy farm in
northern Kosciusko County. The landlord had the dairy barn wired
so the milkers could milk the 30 cows. Much to his credit he thought
that we as his tenants were also worthy of the convenience of electric
lights in the house.

Mother was overjoyed. She hoped that now she could get some

electrical labor-saving devices and appliances. Of course, this was a knotty problem, for which should be first? Money was scarce, so we just couldn't go to the store and buy all the things we wanted. Mother decided a refrigerator was most important. I remember when we went to town to the well-stocked appliance store. There stood an orderly row of white giants. We admired the General Electric, Philco, Norge and Frigidaire models. Mother chose the Norge.

Soon the refrigerator had an honored place in the northeast corner of the kitchen, and was probably the first thing anyone saw when entering that room. Now, no more frequent trips to the cool basement to fetch our milk, eggs, butter of any other food that needed to be kept cool. Now it was just a few steps from the kitchen table to our gleaming white electric refrigerator. Wonder of wonders, this appliance could make two dozen ice cubes in its small freezing compartment, and had enough space one-half gallon of ice cream. But who had money enough to buy that luxury? With milk and cream from our cows, plus eggs from our laying hens we made small batchers of yummy ice cream.

For breakfast we all loved bacon, eggs and toast, so our next purchase was a gleaming chrome Toastmaster. My younger brother and I were the "pop-ups," as we had to manually push the break down and then push the toast up when we thought it was the desired crispness. Since we had too many slices ranging from light to burnt offerings, Papa took over the job as toast master. We enjoyed that hot toast which made the butter melt.

In those days we washed clothes in a wringer washer, making clothes very wrinkly. Ironing took a good part of the day. When Mother got a new Sunbeam electric iron the job became so much easier. This iron felt so lightweight, gliding over the clothes smoothly. No longer did she have to fire up the kitchen range to heat up the heavy irons, and especially in the summer the kitchen was cooler.

Mother often remarked how much she appreciated the labor-saving electric appliances as they continued being added during the coming years. One of the last things added was an indoor bathroom. We were rich now!

I enjoy telling family members about these electrifying experiences.

Karen Y. Hoover
Goshen, Indiana

Snapshots of a Farm Life

When I think of "home" my mind automatically goes back to my grandfather's farm in New Paris, Indiana. It was home for the first 12 years of my life. I was born in Goshen in 1946, the first child and daughter of my young parents. We lived in a little yellow house on Grandpa's farm, but then moved into an apartment above the garage attached to the big farmhouse, and finally into the big farmhouse itself.

Looking back on those years, I have fond memories, memories that poke themselves through my thoughts whenever I least expect them. And just as the copious number of photos my father took help me remember, I would like to share a few "snapshots" of my life on the farm.

I remember steering the tractor (a big red Farmall) carefully down the rows with the hay baler behind and a wagon behind the baler. Daddy helped me turn the tractor at the end of each row. After filling the wagon with bales, off we'd go to the barn where my job was to watch the bales go up the auger to the hay mow. That hay mow was so much fun to play around, climbing the ladder from the thresher floor then climbing the stacks of bales and hiding in them. As children we didn't mind the dust nor the itchiness of the hay!

There was a two-story broiler house on the farm where the new baby turkeys were housed until they were ready to go outside. Seeing the new little baby chicks huddled, chirping, in their boxes was always exciting. But after they'd grown enough to be put outside, both floors of the broiler house would be cleaned out and scrubbed for the next batch of baby chicks. Then what fun it was to ride my bicycle round and round on the concrete floor!

In one end of the barn we kept 200 laying hens. One of my chores was to gather the warm eggs from under the protective hens. The eggs were taken to the basement of the house, to the "egg room," where I helped grade them after they were washed. As the eggs rolled down the chutes of the egg-grader—where they were separated into small, medium, large and extra-large—I packed them into egg cartons. The eggs were then ready to take to market in South Bend every Saturday morning.

Washing down the tall which cupboards in the kitchen every Saturday while listening to "Back to the Bible" with its continuous adventures of Danny Orlis is another memory.

Home included not only my siblings and grandparents. My grandfather was host to "Fresh Air" children from Chicago every summer. He invited a refugee Ukrainian family of six to live in the little yellow house and help out on the farm, and we always had hired hands, students from Bethany Christian High School (which opened in 1954) who needed room and board. The Bethany students provided lots of entertainment, from challenging my father to one-on-one basketball games on the threshing floor to arm wrestling at the dining room table to leg wrestling on the living room floor. One of them had a glass eye that he'd periodically take out to clean.

There was a train boxcar set up on railroad ties out by the broiler house that was used to store chicken feed. What fun to crawl around underneath, in and around, and to climb the ladder built on the side to get to the roof!

There was a butcher house where women my grandfather hire would come once a week to butcher the chickens and turkeys for market. It was always bloody and feathery.

There was a "crick" (creek) running through the farm where I would go to look for unusual "treasures." Once I found a bone that I was sure was a human bone.

There were big ovens in one corner of the garage where every fall we'd make apple butter. Mmm!

In late summer of 1957 my brother, age six, and my uncle, age five, decided it would be fun to light firecrackers in the hay mow. The resulting fire "roasted" the 200 laying hens in one end of the barn, two calves in the calves pen and some farm implements. All that was left standing after burning for two weeks was the silo.

My grandfather sold the farm and my parents, three siblings and I moved to a rural are in the "thumb" area of Michigan. My father never farmed again.

I am now living back here in Hoosierland after being a Michigander since 1958. My parents retired down here in 1992 and Daddy died about two years ago. I bought my parents' condo, but it won't ever be "home." Too many people are missing!

Marian E. Hostetler
Goshen, Indiana

The Store

My father and mother, Harry and Esther Hostetler, had both taught in one-room schools near Orrville, Ohio before their marriage in 1927. When they married, they purchased an IGA grocery store from Dad's brother Chauncey in the small village of Burton City, three miles from Orrville. It was the only business in town. The store had an attached house where we lived. We could go into the store via our kitchen door. Beside the door, in the back of the store, was the wooden roll top desk, Dad's place to do business.

Two of my sisters and I (I was the second oldest) worked in the store as we were growing up. How different it was from today's supermarkets! It was a general store, for we sold gasoline as well as items like men's work shoes and boots, and in the back of the store Dad had a barber chair and equipment he used for giving haircuts. We sold chewing tobacco, pipe tobacco, cigars and papers for rolling cigarettes, though apparently as Mennonites there was a line drawn against selling the actual cigarettes.

Dad had a big wooden table for cutting meat, and a larger cooler for the uncut meat. The cut meat was displayed in a meat case with a glass front. But as for "lunch meat," it was in large pieces, and we had an electric slicer to slice it. The meat was all weighed, according to how much the customer wanted, by placing it on a piece of waxed paper on a scales, then wrapping it in butcher paper which was held shut by a piece of paper tape run through water to moisten the glue on its back. This part resembles today's delis.

We had a pop cooler (the bottles stood in cold water, no cans then) and an ice cream freezer for cones or for packing pints or quarts of the bulk ice cream in wax-cardboard cartons. Vegetables and fruits were in a cooler, but all in bulk, and needed to be weighed and bagged (brown paper bags, no plastic). Milk was delivered daily in bottles from Smith Dairy in Orrville; also bread was delivered daily. I remember three brands—Tastee, Wonder and Nickles.

I think Dad was in the forefront of changing to a self-serve store. He purchased carts so that customers could wheel them around to get their own groceries and installed check-out counter. Before that we clerks would need to get the things customers wanted and place them on a counter. Clerks still had plenty to do though, with the weighing, packaging and figuring up the bills. Many customers had charge accounts, so we had to write everything purchased, item by item in books with a carbon paper page for each customer. We learned to add and make change, for cash registers then didn't do it for you. Later we had a little adding machine.

World War II brought complications. All food was rationed and people had ration books and couldn't buy any more than they had stamps for. Gasoline was also rationed and cars had stickers A, B or C that indicated how much gasoline there were allowed to buy.

The store kept us all busy, but Dad hired other clerks too, high schoolers from our little town. One young Burton City man, Steve Curtis, who had worked for Dad many years until he was drafted into the Army in World War II, later bought the business when Dad decided to sell it after 25 years and move to Orrville to a less strenuous job in his father-in-law's insurance office. I was in college by that time. But "the store" and memories of it remain a part of me.

Mary Kauffman
Middlebury, Indiana

Children Are a Heritage

I was born in West Virginia to a welfare family of two boys and two girls. Father was an alcoholic and a coal miner. Mother was quiet and very submissive. When my younger sister was born, mother died from questionable reasons. My grandma then took my sister and me to live with my uncle. My uncle already had four children and could not afford to care for us. My uncle told me the hardest thing he has ever done was when he carried me to the Orphan's Home. I was two years old. My brothers were six and four at the time.

I was at the Orphan's Home for three years when an Amish family adopted me. At the time there was no cost for adoptions. The Amish family came from Ft. Wayne, Indiana to Maryland to adopt a girl. My family had no electric, telephone, bathroom or running water. The bathroom was an outside toilet. There was a hand pump in the kitchen for water. For clothes, Mom made all our dresses and aprons. She would buy very little material for clothes.

I started going to a Lutheran parochial school when I was six. The school was three miles away and we had to provide our own transportation. The school was a one-room building with all eight grades. We had to learn German and the Bible along with other subjects.

We had an 80-acre farm. There were plenty of chores to do. The milking was done by hand and the milk and cream had to be separated to make butter and cottage cheese. One day my brother and I had a fight so Mom locked us in a smokehouse. It was about four by six feet and pitch black. We kicked and screamed until we were let out. I think that is why to this day I get claustrophobia.

My folks left the Amish and joined the Conservative Mennonites after I had graduated from the eighth grade. After they left they were shunned by the Amish. My father was ordained into the ministry and continued for 33 years. After that I was known as a PK (preacher's kid). Whatever I did was always worse than what the other teenagers did. As I look back, it was a challenge for me as I never wanted to hurt my parents.

At 14 I got a job in Ft. Wayne working for a doctor. They had five children and I did the housecleaning and taking care of the kids. Every day was run on routine. I would get there Monday morning and work until Friday at 4 p.m. I started by earning $8 a week and after eight years was earning $50 a week. It all went to my parents.

In 1943 we move to Middlebury, Indiana and Pop built a house. I started working in a grocery store in Middlebury. At the time many items were rationed because of World War II.

I got involved in the Griner Mennonite Church and met a girl with whom I became very close. She had a brother who was in Civilian Public Service (CPS), serving as a conscientious objector to the war. He came home on furlough just before Christmas. The young folks had a Box Social before Christmas. In a Box Social the girls fix a lunch and put it in a box with enough food for two. Each girl fixed a box to be the prettiest. The guys would bid on the box they wanted not knowing whose box it was. My girlfriend told her brother, my husband-to-be, which one was mine. He paid $22 for the box I made. He only made $15 a month at the time.

We were married on a Sunday morning at Griner Church. At the time weddings were held on a regular Sunday morning. We were not allowed a white dress. We had 300 guests for a full-course dinner with choices of cakes and pies. Two weeks later we went on our honeymoon out west. The honeymoon was a gift from my parents. Our first child was born nine months after we were married and the second child was born two years later.

In 1951, I decided to try to find my biological family. I contacted my older brother and he told me my father's name and the town in which he lived. My husband and I with our two children went to West Virginia. We found my father and he told us about his mother, my grandmother. We went and saw my uncle who had taken us to the orphanage. He had a very nice family but they were very poor. About two months after we returned home, my grandma wrote and wanted to live with us. I never answered. I never told my parents where I had been.

In the next three years I had two more girls. After that we decided on foster care. During the years in foster care we adopted several girls. During the 25 years of foster care, we have had about 50 girls. For 15 of the 25 years I also ran a day care at which I cared for my grandchildren and other children.

I was once asked to write something about adoption, and include that here.

Could You Love Baby?

Could you love a baby?
Any baby? Or just your baby?
Could you love any child or just your child?
You may say, certainly, I love all children.
Mixed race?
You may say, I feel sorry for all children. (You do?)
How sorry?
Sorry enough to open up your heart and home for them?
You might say, But think of all the problems, when they reach
    adolescence or their teens.
Did God promise you would never have problems with your own
    children?
It isn't bearing a child, which necessarily causes a mother to love her
    child.
Love comes as you are with that child, in caring for him or her.
There would NOT be so many children going astray if
childbirth guaranteed that the mother would always love the child.
The Bible says: Lo, children are a heritage of the Lord.

Steve Kruse
Elkhart, Indiana

Got Knob Grass?

The Bainter family on my mother's side and the Kruse family on my father's side are long-time residents of Elkhart County, Indiana. Some might say we come from a long line of farmers proud to have the fertile soil of Indiana farmland under their fingernails.

My grandfather Harry Bainter was a dairy farmer who raised Guernsey cattle on his farm at the top of the hill along State Road 14 South in Bristol. He was attuned to the nuances of nature and the predictability, as well as the random nature, of events. It was he who taught me the old tenets of farm lore.

"Plant your peas on St. Patrick's Day and your potatoes on Good Friday," he told me; advice that factored in the time of the year and a reasonable expectation that the weather would be suitable. Others of his sayings, like plant root crops during the dark of the moon and tall crops in the light of the moon, were more subjective and open to question. But he had an instinct that all good custodians of the land and their animals always have, along with the ability to pick up a handful of soil and tell you what it needed or what would grow best in it.

My mother, Harriet Bainter, Harry's daughter, went to work at the Farm Bureau Co-op after high school in the spring of 1950 until 1956. It was there that she met my father Owen Kruse and became a stay-at-home mom. In 1965 she returned to the Co-op to work, until 1970. Meanwhile Owen had managed the Bristol Co-op for 15 years before it burned in 1969. When management decided not to rebuild, his friends urged him to open a much-need feed mill and farm supply business to serve the local community.

In 1970 he converted a barn on the family property on County Road 6 into a feed mill and began custom-mixing feed for local farmers and sold them products to help grow their crops. Over the years he expanded the business. He knew every one of his customers by named and maintained a friendly old-fashioned general store atmosphere. In his later years Harry Bainter would help out in the store, pleased to keep active in farming.

Father was a practical man who'd sell you marigolds to keep insects away from your vegetable garden but remind you the relative strength of that strong-smelling flower was only about two inches, but the bright color made a pleasant sight. His customers relied on him to interpret their needs, even if there was a language barrier. After World War II a number of Russian immigrants had settled on the lush farmland around Bristol. They would come to the store knowing Owen would get them what they needed. A Russian poultry farmer and frequent customer whose English was minimal came to the store seeking "baby chick na-na-na." The farmer pulled a bunch of striped feathers out of his pocket. "Oh," was Owen's reply. "You want Barred Rock chickens." The farmer nodded and grinned broadly. Another satisfied customer.

Father once told a customer that his value-mix seed could grow grass on a doorknob. For years people would come into the store and ask for that "Knob Grass."

In 1985 he and mother retired to Arizona for the winters and sold the business to me. He continued to be involved in the summer season until his death in 1997. His Golden Retriever, Sam, who had been his constant companion, died just six months later. In 2010 the store celebrated its 40th anniversary. We have an annual Open House that is always a festive occasion and we're still doing business with the same care in serving the customers. And yes, we still sell "Knob Grass."

Roberta Carpenter Leonard
Goshen, Indiana

Awakening of a Cold Winter Morning

As a Depression-aged child, I grew up in a drafty old
farmhouse that had never heard of triple-strength windowpanes.
Upstairs, icy blasts rattled loose single-pane windows that glistened
like colorful jewels when passing cars flashed high-beam lights against
the frosted glass. Dime store lace curtains billowed gently with every
blast of cold air from the west, and did nothing to stop miniature
snow banks from growing on window sills. Downstairs, torn strips
of old sheets were stuffed into cracks in unused doors while scraps of
carpet blocked cold drafts from sneaking under them. As days grew
colder, our house shrunk in size and our family grew closer, as rooms
were dusted, swept and then closed off until the arrival of the first
sunny spring days.

I slept knees-to-chin in my long flannel gown, huddled under
a mound of heavy comforters. I wiggled deep into them, forming a
monk's cowl around my neck and over my head, then buried my cold
nose into their soft folds. The hot water bottle, once warm and soft,
grew cold and clammy before I shoved it over the side of the bed onto
the floor! Beneath my windows, tires crunched through snow-covered
ruts that landscaped our narrow country road, and moon-splashed
tree shadows moved across glistening fields next to our house.
Silhouettes deepened as the sun rose to light the dawn of a new day.

I lay quietly, snug under my igloo of blankets, and listened to a
new morning awakening. Below stairs I heard the dull thump of my
mother's solid square heels as they tracked across the worn kitchen
linoleum, followed by the squeal of the tightly coiled spring at the top
of the woodshed door, and the resounding slap as it flew shut behind
her. Mom, working swiftly against the , numbing cold, scooped long
splinters of dry red cobs into her rusted granite pan, then quickly
retraced her steps back through the kitchen and into the living room.

Our stove, with shiny chrome fenders etched in feathery designs and four knobby chrome feet to support it, stood in the idle of two mismatched nine-by-twelve patterned rugs.

The grating screech of metal perked my ears and sent shivers up my spine, as the fire door opening on uneven hinges. The soft thrust of the heavy iron poker stabbed new life into ashy gray colas, as dry cobs brought scarlet flames to dying embers. Soon the quick swoosh of a sudden blaze sucked up the hollow pipe, sent sharp staccato clicks dancing up the chimney, then, as sudden as a sprung trap, stopped. The stove pipe, polished each fall to glossy black perfection, pushed its way through the ceiling into the bedroom next to mine, to send a cozy warmth into the only heated room above stairs.

Now I knew enough heat had been generated to warm the room next to mine, and it was time for me to get about the business of dressing. I dressed quickly, shoving long underwear into heavy tan stockings, ignoring tattletale bumps that marched in ugly ridges around my ankles. I was a prisoner of those loathsome drawers until a late day in spring when my mother finally announced it was warm enough for me to cast them aside.

Downstairs, bundled up in a hat, coat and boots, I made a narrow patch through the snow to the privy which was almost lost among dark shadows of the old smoke house. Inside, I brushed drifted snow from cold hard boards, then came suddenly to life as goose bumps the size of little green peas exploded on my warm flesh! In winter, nobody dallied on trips to the outhouse!

Inside, the fragrant aroma of bacon sizzling in a heavy iron skillet and the hearty smell of fresh-perked coffee, made me feel warm and cozy. The yeasty smell of toasted break and the sound of six eggs cracked on the dull side of a hot skillet before sliding into the melted lard that sizzle in it, whetted my appetite. As a family, we prayed and ate together before starting the routine of a new day.

The sounds and smells of a morning awakening was my winter alarm clock, and I needed no other to announce the birth of a new day.

33

Roberta Carpenter Leonard
Goshen, Indiana

Innocence in the Midst of Turmoil

I did not know until I was nearly grown that I had unwittingly enjoyed a gloriously "deprived" childhood. Nobody explained to the Huron Street kids that we were living only a whisper away from the days of the dark Depression.

Our block, sandwiched between Pike Street and Lincoln Avenue in Goshen, Indiana, was lined with maple trees up one side and down the other. Children played in back yards, side yards and front yards, cars backfired when cranked, came one-to-a-family, and were kept inside of a one-car garage. Men worked, while wives and mothers stayed home and were called housewives.

In the spring I awakened to the sweet scent of cherry blossoms just outside my bedroom window, and watched a robin feed her young hidden among the leaves. Later, I sat on the back steps and watched my uncle Harry eat wormy cherries. Inside, my mother used a metal hairpin to scoop out pits and worms before baking a fresh cherry pie.

When the pits had dried into little brown "peanuts," I put them in a candy sack and offered them to a friend, who promptly tossed a few into his mouth. After my mother got through with me, I fully understood the folly of my deed!

We built miniature castles in sand that was squeezed between our garage and a neighbor's, played hop-scotch on chalk-marked squares and carefully stepped over a sidewalk crack so we wouldn't "break our mother's back." If not lost, a key was used to tighten roller skates onto everyday shoes so we could skate on the sidewalk or in our large, cool basement.

My sisters splashed with me in the wading pool at Rogers Park, ran through the long, cool pavilion and played under the umbrella-shaped roof of the bandstand, while my brothers caught garter snakes in the swampy area across the road. A rare treat for me was to walk uptown with a friend to the Lincoln Theater to see a Shirley Temple movie for a dime.

Another treat was walking through our back yard to Denver Street for a neighbor's seventh birthday party and winning a big fat pencil for dropping the most clothespins into a milk bottle! Later, when walking home from West Goshen School, another neighbor boy stuffed my brand new tam down the sewer on the corner of Lincoln Avenue and Huron Street. My mother angrily marched down the street with a long-handled rake and fished it out.

In the evening, neighbor kids gathered on our front steps to play "Dare, Dare, Double Dare." The overhead streetlight splashed dark shadows across the pavement as I ran across it to a neighbor's house to carry out my "dare" assignment. When I returned I shoved a fresh-baked cookie into Bob's hand, since he was the one who had dared me to swipe it from the cookie jar on his mother's kitchen table!

In the winter we built snowmen, skated on slippery sidewalks, played checkers on red and black checkerboard squares, and read books from the library on Fifth Street. We went upstairs to bed at 8:00, ready or not. Our parents followed at nine, with doors unlocked.

As young kids, we didn't know our father struggled to earn enough to pay bills, keep food on the table and heat in the house. We didn't know our mother took in a boarder for extra money, did laundry for five on a scrub board, patched our clothes, darned our socks, invented new ways to fix potato soup and fed a neighbor who was "down on his luck," while barely being able to provide for her own family. We didn't know we were living in a time people would forever refer to as the Depression, the "crash" of 1929.

Roberta Carpenter Leonard
Goshen, Indiana

Learning to Live in a Dilapidated 1800s House

When I married in 1945, I was young, ignorant and too much in love to know that the farmhouse into which I had moved with my first love was a total wreck! But it didn't take me long to learn that the house, like the farm buildings, had not been changed or improved since they had been built in the 1800s. In spite of that, I lived in the house for six months before I realized the kitchen had not been painted dark green, but was actually blackened from years of smoke from the wood range. At 19, I was not prepared to cook, clean or ask the landlord for permission to change the house he had lived in unmarried for all of his 75 years.

I was a lousy cook. I learned to cook at my husband's expense, while making grilled cheese sandwiches, potato soup and spaghetti on the gas side of the old range. My small kitchen table and an old but beautiful Hoosier cabinet were the only work spaces I had. An iron pipe attached under the kitchen sink rank through a hole in the wall before emptying dishwater in a five-gallon bucket. If not watched, the bucket ran over and soaked the wood platform beneath it. On windy days our water for the house and barn came from the windmill and on still days it came from my husband and myself, via the hand pump under it.

Having an outside privy led us back to the 1800s when the convenience of an inside bathroom was unheard of. This was sorely missed, along with the lack of an inside laundry room. My laundry room was outside in a building that was used to store wood on one side and a wringer washer with two metal tubs on the other. A small wood stove heated water inside of the copper-bottom boiler along with the cold air that came in through the window. Hauling loads of laundry and an infant back and forth to the house was not a matter of choice.

Living in that old house offered little incentive to clean, which meant that I added more clutter to my clutter as I waited for my mother to come along and pick up after me. The dining room linoleum was dark with age, scabbed off in chunks and as porous as a dry sponge. Since the range wasn't safe to use, a square wood-burning stove in the dining room was the only heat we had for our kitchen, living room and two bedrooms. In the winter we hung blankets at both the kitchen and living room doorways. Except for cooking, our winter was spent eating in the dining room, listening to dad's four-legged Philco radio while sitting beside it on straight-legged dining room chairs and sleeping in the bed we squeezed between the stove and outside wall.

Both bedrooms, located off the 15-by-18 foot living room, were 10-by10 foot square, with eight-foot ceilings. The cloth-backed wallpaper was so old it was on attached at four corners, which allowed it to hang a foot lower in the middle. When expecting our first child, I jabbed it with a broom handle to make it come down, but it bounced instead of tearing. Since the landlord refused to get new paper, without his permission we took the old paper off and painted the walls a warm sunny yellow.

In time, two babies share the little room, ran and played in fresh country air, and watched our pet orphaned lamb jump the pasture field into our dining room, the run around the house before jumping out again! This was a simple feat, since the pasture fence was nailed to either side of the house, which made easy access for our little orphan to jump out of the dining room door that opened directly onto the field.

In spite of living in a house that was more shell than substance, our love flourished, good things happened and inconvenience was put into perspective. We were happy while growing a marriage and starting a family in an 1800s house that had once been considered modern by those who had lived there before us.

RoseMary McDaniel
Bristol, Indiana

A Tribute Letter to My Grandfather

January 1, 2013
Solomon Noah Sherwin
County Road 131
Bristol, Indiana

Dear Grandfather Sherwin:
Although I never met you, since you died in 1928, 14 years before
I was born in 1942, I feel I know you very well, from reading the
journal you began in 1800, over 130 years ago, your "Ignorance"
book and many letters. I know the facts of your life: you were both
a farmer and a teacher. Although there are no color photos of you,
I know that you had auburn hair and blue eyes. You were a shy and
sensitive man, with a tendency to be hurt by the thoughtlessness of
others, since you believed in civility and kindness. You confided your
innermost thoughts in your journal, but feared future readers would
think you daft.

I have heard of your love of books and of the room in your
home in York Township near the Bonneyville Mill, filled with your
library of volumes by the famous poets, philosophers and thinkers
of the time, and of those treasured tomes of Irish literature that took
you in spirit to the Old Country you had never known firsthand. I
still have some of those books today. At 27 you had not yet married,
feeling slightly out of step with your contemporaries who had already
settled into a relationship. But you shared your love of the poetry you
had written as well as ones by popular poets of the day with neighbor
Laura Sanger. Your sister Julia married Laura's brother Henry Sanger,
and at 28 you and Laura were married. This meant that each couple's
future children would be "double cousins." You also began your study
of the German language with your Amish neighbors and converted to

Catholicism, the faith of your forefathers in Ireland, since you loved the "grand old Mass."

After only a few years you abandoned writing in your journal, but you kept up your "Ignorance book," your attempt to gain knowledge by recording lines from favorite poems, passages from authors whom you admired and even occasionally adding poem or short essay you had written yourself. Your "scribbles" as you called them, were much admired by the few with whom you shared them, and a local historian speaking to a group of citizens in 1936 remarked that Bristol never had a writer of renown, but that "Solomon Sherwin could have been our writer, if his talent had broken through." I found that paragraph years later in a pamphlet in the Bristol, Indiana library, and thought it a fitting tribute, but one that you would never see.

I like to think that your love of words and passion for literature runs as deeply in my mind as your lifeblood does in my veins. My love of books from childhood and my desire to write even as a five-year-old comes as much from you as does my love of the golden glow that autumn brings to lift my spirits as you said it did yours. Your only child, my own father, told me he would rather have had a new pair of gloves or pants than the books he often received as gifts from you, but my craving for books, reading and putting thoughts on paper is as strong as yours. I wish I could thank you personally for how much it means to me to share even a small part of your talents. You are an inspiration for me, and I will transform the 100 years of letters, photos and family papers you left behind into a lasting tribute to you, so that future generations may learn of you and your life so long ago. It is at the top of my "bucket list."

Gratefully, your loving granddaughter,
RoseMary Sherwin McDaniel

Alvin Miller
Goshen, Indiana

The Surprise Blizzard

It was a beautiful mild morning for December. There wasn't a cloud in the sky. So far that winter there had not been much cold weather that lasted more than a week.

So Oba Miller and his brother-in-law Simeon Miller went to Goshen on the Shoup bus that ran on a regular schedule between the Indiana towns of Topeka, Shipshewana, Middlebury and Goshen. This was convenient for the Amish to get to town and return the same day. They arrived in Goshen at the Olympia Candy Kitchen around 9:00 and strolled down through Main Street, which at that time had all the main stores.

Soon after they arrived it got dark and began to snow. It was not very heavy at first but soon it was very heavy with large flakes. Then about noon Oba decided he needed to get home before it got too heavy and he couldn't get home. He saw Simeon and told him they should get home as Oba's wife was due with a baby at any time. Simeon said he was going to stay in town with their aunt who lived on Second Street right next to the railroad.

Oba made his way to Olympia Candy Kitchen wondering if the bus might be there. It was and Mr. Shoup was there in the restaurant. Oba said he was worried that the snow was getting deep and he thought they should go before they can't get out of town. Oba said he needed to get home as his wife Fannie is due with a baby at any time now. Mr. Shoup agreed and said so was his wife, and maybe they should leave before the scheduled time. So they left, with Oba as the only passenger, going out East Lincoln Street which becomes Route 4. The snow was quite heavy, wet snow which is harder to cut through. The farther they went the more the snow slowed the bus and finally stopped at "Yoder Corner," which is now County Road 35.

Oba decided to walk to his parents' place and borrow a horse to ride the rest of the way home. He had to walk a mile south and two-and-a-half miles east to his parents' farm. This is also known as Fish Lake Road. He rode a horse without a saddle to his house, which was then known as Cable Line Road and now is 100 South, two miles east of the county line between Elkhart and LaGrange Counties. He arrived home late but glad to be home, and his wife Fannie was also glad.

It snowed hard all night and by morning cleared up, but everybody was snowbound. Then Fannie began to have labor pains and Oba called Doctor Peters in Middlebury to come, using neighbor Early Bontrager's phone. The doctor said there was no way to get there, the roads were all snowed shut. But then he said he thought the road is open to Shipshewana and then going south (now State Road 5) should be better, so he was going to try to make it that far.

Oba and a neighbor went out on their road and shoveled through the deep snow from their house to the road coming south from Shipshewana. That was almost two miles. The doctor arrived just in time and the baby boy was born, whom they name Alvin.

This story was repeated so often that I have it memorized to this day. Often when people ask when I was born I'd ask if they remember the blizzard of '29 Christmas. That's when I came into this world.

B.J. Miller
Goshen, Indiana

A Sod House on the Prairie

In 1929, my parents, Billie and Ada Miller, bought a farm in
Comanche County, Kansas, with dreams of living there one day.
To make that possible Dad had to continue teaching in one-room
schools for a time in order to make payments on the land and provide
for his family. Things became much harder just a few years after
this purchase when the Great Depression hit the country. The rains
stopped and the dust began to blow across the Great Plains, making
living from farming in southwestern Kansas most difficult, especially
for small-acreage farmers.

The farm was just south of Protection in the Collier Flats area,
and Dad's teaching positions were in central Kansas. Our family
would go out to the farm in the summer when school was out, live
in the four-room house on the property and make repairs on the
farm in preparation for the future move. My uncle Harold and aunt
Hazel's family also lived in the area, but from 1932 to 1935 Harold
had little work and no home for the family, so my parents offered
their farmhouse for the winter months. During the summer, though,
Harold's family needed to move out when we came down to work.
Harold and Hazel did have an old cook shack on their 40-acre Bar-M
Ranch, but it was not adequate for their growing family. There was
little money, so in the summer of 1932 the Miller clan in the area
decided to build a sod house for their summer lodging.

A nearby section of the pasture had a wonderful covering of
buffalo grass, which has a thick, deep root system and was often
sued for sod house construction on the prairie. The Miller crew
needed a way to cut the sod into building blocks so, with the help of
blacksmith Kenneth Wimmer from Protection, they built a simple
sod cutter. A metal cutting bar was attached to one end of a two-by-
twelve plank. My cousin Paul Miller remembers that Harold had to

ride on the front of the plan to hold it down as the horse pulled the cutting bar through the sod. They cut out strips of sod four inches deep and 12 inches wide and then cut them into even lengths.

To build the house, the sod lengths were laid grass-side down in a single row, with joints overlapping, similar to the ways bricks are laid. The south wall was built up high enough to accommodate a door and the north wall was lower. The rafters were probably purchased, but they might have been made from cottonwood, mulberry or Chinese elm, the primary trees growing in the area. The roof was made of one-by-twelve in boards overlapped at the lower edge, and bundles of atlas feed were put on top as insulation from the heat. My older brother Chester Miller and cousin Lee Miller both remember "helping" build the sod house when they were six and five years old, respectively.

The outside dimensions were about 12-by-16 feet, and the roof had only one slope. There was a door and possibly a small window on the south side, which was the high side. My cousin Ethel Stutzman remembers that it had a dirt floor and was dark inside. My first-cousins Eugene, Wayne, Lee and Russell Miller all slept in the sod house during the summer from 1932 to 1935, although Russell may have only slept in it the last couple of summers. Lee said that on some really hot nights they slept out in a hay-filled wagon under the stars.

Once most of the repairs were done on the farm, our family would visit for only a few weeks each summer, which meant that Harold's family could live in our house year-round. This was the case from 1936 to 1941. During these visits I remember sleeping with my cousins in the front yard in grass that was taller than my head! I recall the excitement of following paths through the grass to "rooms" with various types of beds, and the fun of sleeping out there with millions of stars overhead and coyotes howling in the distance.

In 1941, when I was eight, our family finally moved to the farm. Since I was only two when the sod house was last used by Harold's family, most of this information about the house is what Lee, Russell, Paul, Ethel and Chester have told me. They all experienced it first-hand in one way or another. It is most interesting to me that in my lifetime my uncle and aunt and some of my first cousins were living in a sod house and a cook shack.

Stephen J. Miller
Millersburg, Ohio

The Dog Biscuits of Life

Living with another person for many years, we develop certain rhythms and routines in our daily lives. Some of those become very tedious and mundane. We don't even think about our actions but just kind of slide along with the flow of daily life. Even the slightest of changes can affect those rhythms, knock you off track, and complete change your outcomes.

I learned from day one that my lovely wife Sara's early morning routine includes a cup of coffee and absolutely no movement, especially talking. My morning before-work routine starts in the kitchen where I grab a dog biscuit from the cupboard, give Sara a quick kiss and wish her a good day. It ends on the porch where our sleepy protector Sandi Claws gets the dog biscuit.

One morning as I began my routine, Sara, coffee in hand, was sitting at the table talking a mile a minute. Unable to get a word in, I laid the dog biscuit in front of her and started toward the door. Not at a loss for words — before I can get to the porch — she said to me, "Are you going to kiss the dog?"

We laughed and laughed about that one for a long time. Of course, one good laugh deserves another, so the next morning as I kissed her goodbye I placed a big chocolate dog biscuit in front of her.

Millie Myers
Goshen, Indiana

My Dad

Daddy reading to us while sitting in an easy chair, with the boys on his lap and the girls on the arms of the chair is a time I remember as a being a warm place to be. Before we went to school we always had devotions. We would sing, Daddy would read from the Bible and then we would kneel and pray.

My mother had many migraine headaches and was not well, so we had hired girls coming in to help. I remember going to the hospital to see mother. She was on the first floor and Daddy helped us climb up on the car roof so we could see her and talk with her. My Mother died of a stroke when she was 36. Daddy's youngest sister, my aunt Lucille, came to live with us until he remarried a year-and-a-half later. I was the oldest of four children. I was 11, Florence was nine, Glen was five and Elvin (Jim) was two years old.

I remember Daddy often helping prepare food to can. He would help snap the beans, shell the peas, cut the corn, make sauerkraut and work with the grapes and tomatoes to make juice. While we did this we would play games and sing songs.

Daddy always had two dogs. He made two carts for them. Two dogs pulled the cart to carry milk from the barn to the milk house where it would cool until time to take it to the cheese factory. One dog would pull the cart he built for two of us to ride. He had also trained the dogs to go get the cows when it was time to milk.

Daddy farmed our 40 acres organically, was also a painter for awhile and then laid linoleum and carpet. He had grown an acre of sunflowers and edible soya beans. He invented a machine to take the seeds off the heads of the sunflowers and also created a machine to shell sunflower seeds. He also liked to experiment in the kitchen.

We had a big gas dryer where he dried fruit and corn to sell as roasted cornmeal. We all helped in the mail order business. We sold

NuMeal cereal, shelled and unshelled sunflower seeds, dried fruit and roasted cornmeal. He advertised in the magazine that is now *Prevention*. Shelled sunflower seeds were a novelty then.

We had two mules instead of horses and a Crosley Jeep instead of a Ford. Florence and I helped drive the mules with the wagon while Daddy loaded the wagon with hay and wheat for the mow. We also helped to shock the wheat. Because we didn't wear jeans our legs got scratched.

We ate mostly off the farm. For meat we ate only chicken and fish. We used raw sugar and gluten flour instead of white flour. I remember going to the grocery store one time with Daddy. I don't recall getting groceries but we brought home a quart of ice cream. What a treat!

I don't remember ever going to a doctor. If we were sick we went on a fast. Daddy was quiet but firm and I don't recall ever being spanked. He never talked about anybody. We liked to hear him sing "No, Never Alone" as he played his guitar.

Some Saturday afternoons we would take a lunch and have a picnic close to a creek. Then we would go into the water for a "swim." We usually came out with blood suckers on our legs. When we were older Daddy would stop working 10 minutes before dark and play softball with us. He would bat the ball and we would catch the grounder or flies.

One Wednesday night Daddy was going to hear a man from Mississippi talk at our church. I wanted to go along. Daddy said, "No, but I will teach you how to spell Mississippi." He wrote it on the green board that he had made for us to use as a chalkboard. It was portable, on wheels, and you could write on both sides.

When Daddy couldn't sleep at night he would get up and write on three-by-five colored paper. He had a big drawer full of his neatly filed notes.

On Halloween he would invite the neighbor children to come and husk corn. Then he would go into the house and start a batch of taffy. We came in from the field, washed our hands and pulled taffy. Pulling taffy with someone else was fun. Because he started with molasses the taffy was dark brown, but after we had pulled it for awhile it was tan. Everybody took taffy home with them.

We have decided that Daddy was 50 years ahead of his time.

Carol Parker
Walnut Creek, Ohio

Our Farmhouse: Every Animal's Habitat

The theme of "Home & Habitat" immediately reminded me of our farmhouse that *was* the habitat of a a parade of animals through the years when we spent two or three days a week plus vacation time there. Maranatha Farm, as we named it, had a farmhouse built in 1888 of the trees cut right there on the 228-acre farm. Alternating strips of white oak and red maple wainscoting decorated the two front rooms. The house was built following the pattern of earlier 19th century homes of the area, in a "T" pattern. Behind the two front rooms, a dining room and kitchen formed the vertical member of the T, flanked on either side with long porches that sometime during the century had been enclosed. We soon commandeered the parlor to be the master bedroom.

In 1890 the husband of the family was killed by a "widow maker," the local idiom for a loose branch that flew out from a tree during timbering operations. The wife, expecting her fifth child, hitched the horse to a farm sled to retrieve his body. Until we bought it, the farm had been occupied by the same family, seldom having an adult male to manage the farm and repair the house. While living in our truck camper we cleaned, repaired and restored the farmhouse and gardens. It was all a labor of love in central "Almost Heaven" West Virginia.

We like our address of Mountain, West Virginia, but found most of our neighbors still called it Mole Hill. In the late 1940s a large evaporated milk company that wanted to put in a processing plant got the named changed. When the deal fell through after the name change, it left our "bend in the road" with the name of Mountain.

A parade of animals lived under that house. Barn cats had kittens, skunks came for vacation and dogs passing through stayed a few days. The animals living inside were more determined to stay. Every night the mice climbed the back of our Hoosier cabinet looking for crumbs in the drawers. There weren't many, but they left their "calling cards" anyway. The mice's specialty was pulling insulation out of the back of the kitchen range. A determined squirrel chewed a hole in the front fa ade of the house, into the space between the floors, to find storage for their winter supply of walnut and hickory nuts. So began their *very* early Saturday morning weekly bowling league. Back and forth they rolled these "balls" in the ceiling over our bed.

Periodically dozens of mice had hysterics in the walls and ceilings. All the running and "screaming" almost gave me hysterics myself. We learned the cause when a well-fed snake dropped down with a thump inside the wall behind my husband's recliner as he relaxed in front of the Franklin stove. One evening, a bat tried to work its way under the closed stove door. One got loose in the house and buzzed my head whenever I played my keyboard in the evening. A short time later, we noticed what appeared to be dry leaves stuck to the drapes, that turned out to be dead baby bats. Eeeeek!

My husband saw the tail end of a snake disappearing through the kitchen door. He pulled it out by the tail, swung it around as he went down the drive and threw it over the bank into the bottom land. Another day he reached for the attic light switch in the dark and quickly pulled back his hand as he sensed something there. A snake was curled around the switch box.

We were both hoeing corn when my husband asked me to get him an iced tea. When I returned he had killed the snake he had spotted ahead of me in my row. Whenever I tell this story to a group of women there is invariably one who says she would tell her husband to get his own iced tea. And I reply, "Then you would have had to deal with the snake."

A large deer herd roamed the farm and targeted the garden, a bobcat came nose-to-nose with my husband and groundhogs climbed our fruit trees for their "apple a day." Squirrels climbed the old pear trees and bi off pears to drop to the waiting deer. A coon jumped into the garden, cut a corn stalk and used it to short out the electric fence and invite the deer in for a feast.

After 22 years we moved to a new house on the banks of the Ohio River with a whole new cast of wildlife. But that's another story.

Leslie Reid
Walnut Creek, Ohio

Mystery in the Meadow

Evening shadows were descending, the twilight sun casting a haunting aura over the pond. Gazing southwestward through the wide windows of her comfortable living room, Jean beckoned her husband saying, "What do you suppose that is up on Levi's hillside?" Slowly setting aside his sherry glass, Les shuffled across the room to gain a suitable viewpoint. "Can't really tell from here, but I do see something up there. Fetch me the glasses, would you dear?" Removing his bifocals Les adjusted the field glasses as he trained them on the target.

"My word!" he exclaimed. "It looks like a dead duck. I can make out what looks like its head and, oh my, it seems to be moving! Here, take a look." Jean readjusted the focus and peered at the mysterious sight. "I can't really identify it," she said, "but part of it does seem to be moving a bit." Les wondered, "A duck, or what else could this possible predator be?"

Les thought for a moment and then suggested that he should call George, who with his wife Polly lived 150 yards to the south and would have a different view. George picked up and after Les identified himself he explained the strange and mysterious things that were going on in their backyards. Maybe George would take a look at the apparition from his window. George obliged without hesitation and soon reported back on the phone that "Yes, indeed there is something out there but it definitely is not dead, for I can make out movement." Following a brief deliberation George said, "Hang on Les, I'll just step out and take a closer look."

"Be careful, George," Les said. "It could be almost anything," adding to himself "or anyone."

From his living room window Les watched as George's garage door crept open and in the early evening's dimming light Les observed the carefully clad figure of his neighbor, with dark jacket and protective hat to share his figure, carrying a "sure grip" long-handled round-nose shovel. "Good thinking, George," Les thought to himself. "Protect yourself against any possible menacing unknown." With cautious steps George slowly approached the dark and unidentified mystery phenomenon. Stopping but a few feet away from his target, George, in what his friend could only construe as a move of bravery, raised his shovel overhead and in one fell swoop impaled the once-moving figure.

Regaining his poise and slowing his anxious breathing, George used his implement to pick up the now inert specimen. From his window Les observed that his friend was now making his way toward Les' house with his trophy carried high on the blade of his shovel. Fearing that the awful remains would be deposited on or close to his front porch, Les pulled on his slippers and hastened to meet George as he approached.

The moment of truth was about to be revealed. What mystery did this shovel blade bear?

In the now darkened evening George, with considerable ceremony, deposited his mysterious quest at Les' feet and declared that "The Mystery in the Meadow" could be considered solved. Les, in disbelief, gazed upon what had absorbed and somewhat traumatized them for a good part of the evening. A billowy black plastic trash bag!

Wes Richard
Goshen, Indiana

Life's Boundaries

I grew up in a home where humor and discipline were a part of our family life. Even now, after retirement, I can recall fun family Christmas projects when father and children together fashioned a Christmas gift of grocery items for Mother. As children, we delighted in this little secretive scheme of using foodstuffs to create the shape of a two- or four-legged animal as we carefully wrapped each can and bottle with paper and then stacked or taped them together and placed them under the Christmas tree. And, of course, Mom responded with joyful surprise. That bit of Christmas humor has now been passed on to the next generation. The most recent such grocery gift came to us assembled with unusual items from Trader Joe's.

Some practical jokes originated outside our household. Once, when our family came home from an evening away, we found that some prankster had somehow managed to corral several of our barnyard cats and put them inside our house. Another time, my parents found hard, uncooked macaroni between the sheets on their bed after their wedding anniversary party. My dad suspected someone from his Sunday School class, so the next day he wrapped the macaroni in a box, along with a few heavy bolts and washers and, perhaps with just a twinge of revenge mixed with humor, he sent it postage-collect through the mail, when that service was still available.

After my dad became a pastor, he and Mom invited a young couple, newly added to the church, to our home one evening. I'm sure it was my dad who challenged Jack to an ice cream eating contest. Counting by number of dips, which Dad provided from the gallon container, he soon overtook Jack by a considerable margin. What Jack didn't know until later was that his dips were solid while his competitor's were hollow! I can still hear Dad's humorous recounting of the event to the rest of us afterwards.

While family life was a lot of fun, I learned that pushing the boundaries would not be tolerated. I was told before starting my formal education that if I ever got a spanking at school I could expect one at home. Soon after beginning kindergarten at Wayland (Iowa) Public School I transgressed by running in the basement hallway as I hurried to the restroom. My teacher, Miss Ritter, made sure I understood the rule from that point on by applying a ping-pong paddle as her board of education. That evening my dad further etched the importance of obedience on my behind.

Soon after receiving my first new bicycle, the excitement of speeding all around the farmyard overcame my desire for doing my chores. One day when I got home from school I found my green machine hanging by a rope in the southwest corner of the machine shed, an indignity I bore for a whole week.

At other times of misconduct, I experienced grace. On my ninth birthday I was permitted to invite three or four boys from my class home with me to celebrate. At dusk, as my friends and I walked about out in the yard, I found a stray softball near our big elm tree, so I threw it toward the house so it wouldn't get lost.

Unfortunately, the ball traveled beyond its intended landing place, bouncing on the porch and then crashing through the kitchen window, rolling across the extended table Mom had prepared for the birthday meal. To my shame, I continued walking around outside with my friends as though nothing had happened. When we went into the house for the meal, I saw that the window opening had been covered with a big piece of cardboard. My mother had cleaned the broken glass off the table and out of the jam dish and had changed the tablecloth. Maybe Mom thought I had learned my lesson; she allowed the party to go on as though nothing had happened. I don't recall getting scolded or punished. But I felt guilty and, eventually, I apologized.

One other time, my own carelessness served as sufficient punishment when I forgot to close the lid on a cage that held my white pet rabbit. I never found the rabbit and could only imagine what a terrible fate it must have met.

As I reflect on my childhood, I realize that home is where the concepts of justice and mercy were instilled in my life because of the way my parents treated me. Even though my mother once wrote that she felt that as parents they may have "failed at times to train their children in the right way," I can only be grateful for their attention to life with boundaries.

Bonnie L. Smith
Goshen, Indiana

I Was Young Once

Memory is a wonderful thing, and growing old isn't so bad. It surprised me sometimes what things can take me on a trip down memory lane. Just the other day I stopped at a restaurant to get an order to go. I was sitting there waiting on my order and watching these "young," "slender" and "pretty" waitresses hurrying about, taking food to that table and clearing off another. I sat there and though, "I was young once...."

I was young, I was slender and I was pretty. In 1945 I was 16 and worked in a restaurant and I could hurry from table to table. I remember my pay was 25 cents an hour and tips were unheard of.

I grew up in a family of six girls and one boy; counting my mother and father there were nine of us. Our house had one bedroom on the first floor and two bedrooms on the second floor. This house had no running water, which meant we pumped all the water that we used. The pump was on the back porch and there was a path to the outhouse. We had a coal stove sitting in the living room and daily after school we carried in a bucket of coal and some kindling wood. I always wondered how Mother kept all her things in one old-fashioned cabinet. I was young back then....

I was young when my sister Wilma and I walked about a mile back and forth to school together in rain or shine. Some days we picked up pretty autumn leaves and other days we lay down and made angels in the snow. I was young once....

I was young when my girlfriend and I went to Elkhart Roller Rink to skate. I saw this guy who could really skate well and I told my friend that I would like to skate with him. He came over and asked me to skate. We were both young. We skated often to beautiful organ music under a circling strobe light and never fell down. We had the happiness of being together for 60 years.

We were young when we got married and borrowed $125 for our first bedroom suite. We purchased it from my girlfriend's sister-in-law. It was beautiful, just like new. It was complete with bed and mattress, chest of drawers and a vanity with a large octagon mirror and a vanity bench. We pad the loan back $10 per month.

I was young but so happy when we moved into our first apartment. It was upstairs and just three rooms and a bath. Our rent was $15 each week.

I was young when I walked about two blocks to catch the city bus to go to work at Penn Electric, which was later Johnson Controls.

We were young when we purchase our first new home in 1951 for $6,300 and paid for it at $45 a month. This was a brand new prefabricated home with three bedrooms and one bath. My husband made scalloped cornice boards for above all the windows and build in a towel cabinet. He later built on a garage and a breezeway. We were happy and had three children while we lived there.

When we sold that house my husband and his brother built us a nice, larger house. It had three bedrooms, one-and-a-half baths, full basement and attached garage. It had lots of cabinets and closets. One closet was just right for the sweeper, ironing board and hooks that were just the right height so the children could hang up their coats. While living there we had our fourth child. We were young, happy, contented and blessed of the Lord.

The children grew up, they got married and have families of their own. Now I am a grandmother and a great-grandmother. I am not young anymore. I like being a grandmother and great-grandmother. I like seeing my children happy and hearing all the cute things the little ones do.

I decided when I became a great-grandmother to never say I'm getting older. I tell people I am getting "greater"; that sounds so much better.

Is it really true that it is a sign of old age when you can remember the past so vividly?!

Bonnie L. Smith
Goshen, Indiana

The Little House Down the Lane

In the early 1900s during the Depression, there was a little house down the lane. In this house was a father, mother, a son and six daughters. In this little house there were happy times and sad times. There was another baby boy but he died at birth. That was a sad time.

The father went to work. The mother cleaned, cooked and did the laundry. In the winter the wet clothes were hung on a rope that was strung around the living room for them to dry. She kept everything clean. This family did not have much of this world's goods. In fact, they were very poor. They all worked hard and were content.

This little house had three bedrooms. The brother had his own room and the sisters shared. There were times their mattresses were straw ticks with clean straw every time wheat was harvested. They had a pump on the back porch that had very good drinking water. They pumped and carried all the water that they used. No indoor plumbing, just a path to the outhouse. They did have electricity, but it was just a cord hanging down in the middle of the ceiling with a light bulb screwed in it that they reached up to turn on.

There was a stove in the living room where they burned coal and wood. There was a radio on a stand in the living room to which the father listened. The mother sang hymns as she worked in the kitchen. The children played in the apple trees and sang. They did not realize until years later that their neighbors at the end of the lane could hear them and enjoyed their singing.

The sisters did all the dishes in two dish pans on the table. One washed, the others dried and the mother wiped up the floor afterwards. The mother never learned to drive; the children walked to school in all kinds of weather.

This little house was on five acres with a creek on one side. They had a cow, pony, pigs and chickens. The mother would set a hen on some eggs and several weeks later they enjoyed watching the hen with her peeps strolling in the backyard.

They planted corn for the animals. They planted lots of potatoes and when these were harvested they were carried to a bin in the cellar. The whole family worked at planting, weeding and harvesting. The mother canned a lot of fruit and vegetables and was proud of those shiny cans sitting on the shelf in the cellar. They had gelatin desserts in the wintertime. Since they had no refrigerator they put a lid on the gelatin and set it in the snow to jell.

In that little house one little girl at the age of five was accidently shot. They drove her to the hospital, where she was for several weeks and did survive. The town people took up a collection to help pay the hospital bill. One little girl tripped over her shoestring and broke her leg but the doctor set it and she healed nicely. One little girl broke her arm when she toddled behind a car.

The brother was riding his pony in the field one day when it decided to lie down and roll. He hung on and received a bad gash on the top of his head. There was no 911 to call in that day and they did not have a telephone, so the mother cleaned the cut and it healed.

The men back in that day made homemade dandelion wine. The mother was doing the laundry when one of the little girls took a drink of the wine and liked it. She had several more tastes and the next thing the mother knew that little girl could not walk straight. At the same time a woman who had sewed a dress for that little girl came to try it on her. The little girl had trouble standing up. Oh, what an embarrassing time for that mother!

The children grew up and married. The sisters each remember when she stood at the kitchen window and watched for the car lights as her boyfriend drove down the lane. In 1947 the father died suddenly of a heart attack. Several years later the mother married again and moved away from the little house down the lane. That little lane is paved now and there are homes instead of farm land. The members of the family still love to drive slowly down the lane and reminisce about their growing-up years when they lived in the little house down the lane.

Arleta Unzicker
Goshen, Indiana

Scenes of My Childhood

Our 10-acre woods helped to heal the pains of childhood and
adolescence. After rounding up the cows on a summer afternoon,
we could perch on the wood pile that represented Dad's own way
of retreating and luxuriate in the richness of the woods. We drank
in the scents of pennyroyal, grass, dry leaves and wood. Bobwhites,
meadowlarks from the adjoining fields, mourning doves, blue jays
and other birds we couldn't identify improvised symphonies.

Of course, on damper days mosquitoes would zing around our
faces in their abrasive fashion, and sometimes the cow smell lingered
after the cows had left or a worm crawled out of the woodpile, but
these were minor distractions. Sometimes, before following the cows
through the lane toward the barn, we picked some pennyroyal for
tea afterwards or some wild roses, tokens of carrying the woods back
with us.

In the fall we took off for the woods to gather hickory nuts
and colored leaves. One leaf of ever y kind and color made a good
collection.

One brief winter interlude in the woods left me with a memory
I will always treasure. It was February. I headed for the thornapple
tree for some little branches. I wanted to put gumdrops on the
ends of the two-inch thorns and hang heart-shaped paper leaves on
the branches I intended to pain white. A foot of snow covered the
ground. Several inches clung to every branch. No wind stirred. Huge,
fluffy flakes fell without a sound. It was a beautiful world without a
hint of corruption.

A month later the personality of the woods changed with the
nighttime freezing and daytime thawing. Spring was the season and
maple syruping the sub-season. We loaded up the mud boat with
galvanized pails, bamboo spigots and an augur for drilling. Dad had

to drill holes in the maple trunks, insert spigots and hang buckets on the spigots to catch the sap. I don't remember helping. I do remember listening to the bird calls and enjoying the woodsy scents.

An evening trip to the woods to collect the sap began while it was still light. In my earlier memories the horses, Dick and Molly, pulled the mud boat loaded with Dad, kids and barrels. Later we used the Oliver tractor. We emptied the sap from the pails into the barrels. "I'll get these three. You get those two over there." We had to hurry because it was getting dark fast. There was probably time for a sip or two. Sap right from the tree is a wonderful beverage, sweet and unpasteurized. It gave a stomach ache to anyone who didn't know when to stop.

On the way back, the sap we had just harvested, the plowed ground ready for spring planting and the night air blended their aromas to delight our nostrils. The woods behind us stood now a forbidding mass, and ahead of us the lights of the house and the outdoor fire for cooking the sap to make syrup welcomed us. The air had a chill we didn't notice when we rushed from tree to tree to mud boat and then again from tree to mud boat.

The mercury would drop below 32 before morning and the sap would stop flowing for a few hours. Above us in the sky Orion the Mighty Hunter stood silently, a passive participant in an older sister's show-and-tell astronomy lesson.

Poems

Roberta Carpenter Leonard
Goshen, Indiana
Excellence in Writing—Poetry

The Drought

A river of heat flows across the land as
a summer sun, torrid and unrelenting,
sends incandescent waves dancing from fissure to fissure,
dividing stalk from root and leaf from stem.

Furrows planted with hopes and dreams,
yellow into road maps of dried grass and brittle straw,
while foliage lies wilted upon a barren ground
that proclaims the poverty of the land.

A creek, winding through furrowed fields,
puddles into islands of stagnant, fetid water,
ugly in its crust of floating scum, then
dries and cracks into patterns of wrinkled brown clay.

A farmer prays for rain and searches the skies
for a curtain of darkness, heralded by a cacophony
of thunder and light that splits the clouds and
sends a torrent or rain upon the thirsty land.
But there is only a blazing sun in a cloudless blue sky.

Excellence in Writing—Poetry
Roberta's use of riveting images and strong, sometimes stark, descriptions creates a clear vision of a dry, thirsting land. The words flow yet bite, much like a hot breeze across an arid landscape. It's also a wonderful metaphor for the drought of soul that we sometimes experience. We search for the water of life; will it appear?

Wanda A. Alwine
Goshen, Indiana

I Ain't Dead Yet

My hair is white and I am almost blind, and the days of my youth are
    far behind.
My neck is stiff, can't turn my head, can't hear half that's
    bein' said.
My legs are wobbly, can't hardly walk. But glory be, I still
    can talk.
And this is the message I'd have you get: I'm still a'kickin', I ain't
    dead yet.

My teeth are gone, my dentures new, wobble about when I chew.
My memory is poor, not good at all. So many things I can't recall.
I lost my teeth long, long ago, and my voice is harsh and low.
My muscles ache when the weather is wet. But still I can move 'n' I
    ain't dead yet.

My joints are stiff, won't move in their sockets. And many a dime is
    left in my pockets.
But still I'm having a lot of fun and my heart with joy is overrun.
I've lots of friends so kind and sweet, and seldom more I never meet.
Oh, this is a wonderful world of ours, shade and sunshine and
    beautiful flowers.
So you just take it from me, you bet, I'm glad I'm livin' and I aint'
    dead yet.

I've corns on my toes and ingrowing nails. And do they hurt?
    Language fails.
To tell all my troubles would take too long. Even if I tried, you would
    give me the gong.
I go to church and Sunday School too, for I love the stories that are
    ever and new.

And when I reach the end of the row, I hope to that heavenly home I
    will go.
And when I leave this house of clay, if you listen closely, I'm apt to
    say,
"Well folks, I've left you, but don't you forget, I have passed on, but I
    ain't dead yet!"

*Wanda Alwine wrote this in 1934 when she was 16 years old, for her
mother. The* LaGrange News *(LaGrange, Indiana) printed it then.*

John M. Bender
Elkhart, Indiana

January 1969

Between Toronto and Winnipeg
from sequestered quarters
on CN's precursor to VIA Rail
I window gaze
into woolly forests
frozen lakes
village streets walled with snow;
vast space an echo chamber
for the clatter of steel on steel.
Inwardly I muse
on studies ending
work dawning
the future unfolding;
dreams hushed with hopes
of a happy new year.

Martha A. Burger
Elkhart, Indiana

Mom's Birthday

My mom was a woman who could "make things do,"
from making a dress to mending a shoe.
She canned, she gardened and she knew how to cook,
yet at the end of the day she enjoyed a good book.
She let me read books and she taught me to sew.
She gave me life lessons that I will never outgrow.

She picked the wild berries for pies and for jam;
on butchering day she knew how to cure ham.
She killed water and black snakes with a hoe or a stick.
Once skunk spray in her face made her really sick.

In a big copper kettle she made apple butter.
She dug potatoes, picked tomatoes and used the corn cutter.
She cooked squirrel and deer meat and even groundhog.
For the fire in the cook stove, she helped split the logs.
While Daddy was gone in the far South Pacific
she got a washing machine. That was terrific!
She made laundry soap from lye and from lard;
she stirred it over the fire and let it get hard.

I became a nurse, got married and moved far away;
though she had her doubts, she never said "Stay."
I saw her less often, at least once a year.
My thoughts and my memories still hold her dear.
Almost every week she wrote me a letter.
For keeping in touch, it could not have been better.

Mom and dad stayed on the farm through good times and bad;

she still had a garden and used what they had.
The years went by quickly and her body gave out.
She didn't like that, there was no doubt.

The songs that she sang and the tales that she told,
I now tell my grandchildren, as memories of gold.
Today is her birthday and my memories renew
of my childhood on Reeds Creek
when my Mom "made things do."

Jim Carpenter
Syracuse, Indiana

It's Late Afternoon

The night still seems a far way off,
with many things yet to come my way.
Until my life has filled its purpose,
and God will deem to call it a day.

It is coming on to late afternoon,
In the season of my life.
There's quite a bit of daylight left,
but soon it will become twilight.

And yet, I have spent much of this long day,
chasing after meaningless things.
But all roads lead to the present,
to realize the peace this day can still bring.

The dusk might soon be upon me,
but still there is much to be done.
To finally realize what life can mean,
and to know how far I have come.

You see I have found a path to contentment,
a way to find the peace that God can give.
I have found that in serving others,
I may truly more abundantly live.

To live my life as it was meant to be,
with honesty and purpose and a great deal of love.
Until the day is night and God calls me home,
to the mansion that awaits me, in heaven above.

Jim Carpenter
Syracuse, Indiana

The May Garden

March has the promise of spring.
April has flowers and rain.
But May is the month I love the most,
when the planting can truly being.

The frost-free day will soon be here,
'though carrots and lettuce are up.
But now the tomatoes and peppers go in,
and I wonder, "Will there be room enough?"

With cabbages growing and potatoes showing
the sweet corn is spiking its way.
Soon the beans will start to take off,
what a wonderful time, this month of May!

The sweet potato and zucchini are starting,
not to mention the cucumber vine.
The carrots are coming, the radishes are near,
soon it will be pea picking time!

The month of May has promised galore,
no matter rain or sun.
So when I say I work in the garden,
I'm really out there having fun!

Of all the months that come in a year,
There are none any finer than this.
Scrunching toes in the dirt, feeling the sun,
Surely, this must be bliss!
The days go by, the garden grows,
but this one thing I know:
In the garden, as in our life,
we harvest what we sow!

Lois T. Clark
South Bend, Indiana

The Winter of Our Discontent

Deep within our Planet's Soul
lies life's seed, awaiting spring;
nurturing (despite the present maelstroms of events),
all the values we esteem!

Like the maple, bare of limb,
but life-force growing deep within,
at the core, in every human,
whatever culture, faith or race,
these values await their emerging time to see the Light of Day,
whate'er the color of each face.

Stationing lives on the desert "line"
(lives we've nourished with the best that we know),
teasing Death by hastening His time—
'tis truly the Winter of our Planet's Soul!

Can we convince our leaders to stop the Hell
before the killing begins?
Will we allow this Season's Spirit
to bloom in our hearts and swell
into deeds and acts that will recognize,
before it is too late,
that Winter's bare limbs will leaf again—
if we just have the patience to wait?

This was written the winter the United States went into Iraq. "The beat goes on" in Afghanistan, Pakistan, and on and on. Alack and alas! The planet is my "home and habitat."

Annabelle Herschberger
Millersburg, Ohio

The Change of Seasons

The crisp and chilly autumn breezes
whirl the leaves in spirals up and down,
as if to say, time for a change.
The earth now wears a new gown.
We follow the season down the road;
observe what she has to unfold,
what a wonderful process of colors:
red, brown and gold.
The maple of summer has changed from
green to golden delight.
The hum of tractors reaping harvest,
autumn's fulfillment to height.
We think of another harvest
at the close of time and age;
let's make sure our names are there
on God's best record page.
And as our basements shelves and freezer
are filled up to the brim,
we need to set aside a special day
of praise and thanks to Him!

Roberta Carpenter Leonard
Goshen, Indiana

Mama's Washday

Like a shepherd's crook her back
is bent over a scrub board that is
firmly immersed in a metal tub
of hot, soapy water.

Hands, with square-cut nails,
laboriously knead a cotton dress
against the dull edges of
corrugated metal.

Wispy strands of dark hair escape from
a coiled knot at the nape of her neck
as she wipes at sweat that shines
on her face and trickles down her spine.

Fingers, strong and blunt, squeeze soap
from socks and shifts, then dumps
them into a blue water rinse.
The pungent smell of lye wafts from

Paisley and plaid, as they drip from a gray
rope that sags between splintered posts.
Then, like a shepherd's crook her back is bent
over a small child with a scabbed knee. With
work-worn hands, she holds him close and
croons a lullaby.

This is mama's washday.

*During the Depression this scene was repeated at our house every Monday
morning, until Mom had saved enough money to buy a second-hand
Maytag washing machine for $35.*

Roberta Carpenter Leonard
Goshen, Indiana

Salute to Volunteer Firemen

Sirens trumpet flashing red lights as fire
trucks race along the river road and
jolt to a stop at the end of the narrow lane.
A parade of blue lights follows, while the
water wagon lumbers in the distance.

Ugly in its blackness, smoke spirals and
twists inside the old wood barn.
Flames crack in the eerie stillness,
winding through the airless blanket
of fog, to explore into the gaping black
hole in the roof.

Timbers crash into the smoky gray ash,
spewing red and yellow sparks into a
riotous display of destruction.
A ladder, a hose and an ax. Puny weapons
against the undulating flames that slice
through churning black clouds.

Water gushes and steams as the exhausted men
spray the last dull flames into submission.
Tired and dirty, they kick at burning embers,
and wonder if they could have done more.

Volunteer firemen. Men who work with
diligence and pride for their neighbor,
who can only grasp their hand and mumble a
heartfelt thanks for a job well done.

I grew up hearing and seeing the above scene in both Millersburg and Benton, Indiana. A few young Amish men around Millersburg became volunteer firefighters as their way of showing appreciation to the Millersburg Fire Department for the many times they have been helped during a fire. The poem describes a barn that burned to the ground only a few miles from us.

Roberta Carpenter Leonard
Goshen, Indiana

The Warring Sky

Clouds, as muddy as water paints
sloshed in a pan, drift low, almost stalled
in their journey over the woods, while shards
of light pierce the darkness, and drill relentlessly
into the patchwork of fresh plowed earth, as
a farmer charges through the splinters of brittle
dry stalks. Thunder echoes like a lumbering
freight train as it crawls above the land on the
scent of a rain-coated breeze.

Clouds church angrily, lightning streaks
through the darkening sky, and thunder
rolls like a drumbeat before the oncoming storm.
A high wind dips and soars, then, like vultures,
ominous black clouds gather over the stubble
and rain slashes the earth in unrelenting fury.
In silent protest the laborer yields to the river of
water that swamps the straight dark rows and
drives him home from the field.

Richard E. Martin
Middlebury, Indiana

A Vision of Beauty on a Gray Day

Rainy and gray was the day.
My spirit reflected the day.

Through the kitchen window
I spied a vision of beauty—
a yellow finch swinging
in the lazy motion of
a tree branch.

A hue that was brilliant yellow
on a day that was dull gray.

Thank you, Lord, for a
vision of beauty
on a gray day.

Alta Roth Mellinger
Goshen, Indiana

Cross Cultural Crafts

THE COUNTRY
Crash course Central America
Conquering Columbus came
Catholic cathedrals chimes
Close calls curves chaos
Cockadoodledoo clamor
Cactus critters clutter
Common crime critical
Cynical conflict corruption

THE COMPANY
Capable Canadian couples
Casas' compesinos co-ops
Contras' crisis control
Cooked chicken comfort
Cautious corn consumption
Cramps chills critical
Children crying concerns
Caring compassionate Christians

THE CRAFT PERSONS
Clear coral complexions
Craftsmen commute city
Cotton crops cultivation
Clover comfrey chamomile
Clothes concept completion
Combined construction
challenges
Colorful child carriers
Courage concrete changes

*These word images were penned after a learning tour to Honduras
and Guatemala in 1992 arranged by SELFHELP Crafts of Akron,
Pennsylvania and sponsored by Cross Cultural Crafts store in Glen Ellyn,
Illinois.*

Margaret J. Metzler
Goshen, Indiana

Christmas 1979

If suddenly I could not hear the carols of Christmas loud and clear,
if I could not see the signs of Christmas—holly wreaths and all the
    cheer,
if desert sands instead of snow surrounded me...
        Would it still be Christmas?

If by chance my job should fail,
if all around me too became so poor we could not buy the tinsel and
    the tree,
if those Army bells tinkled for *me*...
        Could there be Christmas then?

Or if a loved one dear and true, whose presence always made
        Christmas special, suddenly was taken...
        Could I, would I know Christmas then?

If my own brother waited out his days in the Veterans' Hospital,
like a prisoner for life, waiting his own death to release him...
        Could I look at him (above his mangled body) and say,
        "Merry Christmas, brother! Times will be good again!
        Cheer up! It's alright! Christmas is here!"

Or if perchance I found myself
pushing, along with others in the line-up for the bus,
or waiting with 87 others for the green light,
looking up at tiny patches of gray sky between 30-story buildings,
just one ant on the hill with millions of others,
        Would I feel Christmas then?

Or if my neighbors in my jungle village home came today.
Their child is ill. High fever wracks the thin small frame.
There is no doctor near. They look at me and say, "You can save
     our child."
I look down at the red and green I was about to hang on the palm
     branch walls for decoration.
I feel helpless.
          What *does* Christmas mean?

Or if crowds of hungry children stared at me
vacantly, their hollow eyes boring into my very soul,
their weak voices crying for bread,
          Would I make my holiday break?

Or, you and I are not alone at home but in a refugee camp.
We came here last April. We fled by boat, a rickety thing,
tossed by storm at seas, not knowing what to dream of for the future.
We have waited in the humid heat for some relief to meet our needs.
Now it is December—the month we have heard Christians say is full
     of joy
(something about the birth of a baby boy named Jesus, God's Son,
     they say).
What does it mean? How can they celebrate, when life's so cruel?
Our fate seems held not in the hands of God, but those of men.

Lord, I know that tinsel and the snow,
the greenery and the candles' glow,
the jolly jingle bells, the cakes and cookies, sacks of sweets,
the Christmas turkey, and other eats,
the buying and the selling,
the rushing and the running,
the coming and the going
          do not make it Christmas.
Please
Take away the things that clutter and blind the body and mind
of all of us at Christmastime.

Help me to act, to reach out in love
as you have reached to me.
Help me to know again
it was not things you gave to show your love to me,
but LIFE, Your own Life—born anew within me—
created again,
Jesus within!

Margaret J. Metzler
Goshen, Indiana

Look Them in the Eye

Crowds of people passing by
each in their own world.
Hundreds of topics in hundreds of minds—
I walk on, keeping to myself.
My own thoughts keep me occupied
in my own privacy.
But… we are all neighbors
if just for this passing moment.
What is our relationship?
Do we hold anything in common?
Can we touch in any way?
"Don't be too friendly…."
"Strangers cannot be trusted…."
"I'm scheduled to get there and cannot take time
        to even look up,
        give a nod of greeting,
        or speak a word…."

I heard of a young woman
who greeted a lone stranger on a bridge.
A beautiful young woman who simply said,
"Have a good day."
He felt touched, warmed
with that blessing for a day.
(He did not jump off the bridge.)
He's living a good life
All because a passerby
took the time
and looked him in the eye.

Henri Lee Richards, Sr.
Nappanee, Indiana

Native American

When the white man came to this great land,
to hunt and fish and raise a family,
he was alone, as far as he could see.
But there was a breed already here,
the Native American that had no fear.

Now they must learn from each other,
so some day, they could call each other Brother.
The path would be long and filled with strife.

But in the end, make a much better life.
For both the white man and the red,
sometimes we followed , sometimes we led.
To the Native American, I have just this to say,

You have had such a high price to pay,
for this land, water and sky so blue,
that has *always* belonged to you.

Daniel Roll
Elkhart, Indiana

The Diary

The Shipshewana Auction draws them in from near and far.
An Amish auction, grossing a million dollars this day with
buyers milling about putting things aside or taking notes
on things they would bid on: antiques, treasures, resale items.

Not for me. It was nothing but the passing of time as my friend
positioned himself for his first bid. His bids suffered for lack,
but he was never discouraged, just moved on to another one.
Buyers picked up items placed on the floor surrounded
        by tape.
 This marked off area was evidently another seller's offerings.
I bent to retrieve a small leather-bound book. Gently used,
yet surrounded by manly things, tools, fuel pumps, oil cans.
The final bid for this little book, I pondered, upon opening it.

I read, written in a feminine hand: "Today is Christmas day!
Momma and I scrubbed the hardwood floors. My papa is
tending the horses, and my brother is helping a neighbor.
We will be going to friends tomorrow. I love Christmas!"

No mention of gifts, Christmas trees or any other traditions.
And yet, the author loved Christmas. Why?, I wondered,.
Because of the spirit of the season, or maybe for the reason of it?
I placed it back in its place on the floor as the auctioneer approached.
"What am I offered? A dollar? Maybe two?" he asked.

Bill Sheldon
Goshen, Indiana

Boat Mates

We pause oft times to reminisce
of good times from the past.
We draw them from the deepest well
of memories, how they last!

It brings to mind a time in life
back when the kids were small.
They led you on a merry chase,
you reveled in it all.

The Lord somehow enabled you
to fill each busy day,
to feed and scrub four precious kids
and send them on their way.

Samson, Job and Solomon,
their gifts combined in one,
are found in youthful motherhood;
that's how you got things done.

But now you ask what's happened
to your capabilities,
why it takes so long to do the tasks
that once were just a breeze.

You did things like a whirlwind then,
come problems or what may,
but now the only thing that's fast
is passage of your day.
You ask, "What's wrong with me of late?
Is it just me alone
who finds intentions good, but then,
alas, the day is gone?"

If morning's goals are still unreached
when falls the evening dew,
move over, mate, lend me an oar.
I'm in the same boat, too!

Erma N. Yoder
Goshen, Indiana

December Questions

It's winter, and I'd like to know—

Those flowers out there beneath the snow
that grow and bloom with colors bold,
how can they sleep when it's so cold?

Those geese that flew in a perfect vee
to a destination that they can't see,
I've often wondered, how do they know
in a sky so vast, just where to go?

And little sparrows with songs so sweet,
why don't they freeze their tiny feet?

These are all a part of the loving design
of the Heavenly Father, yours and mine.

Erma N. Yoder
Goshen, Indiana

STUFF

Where
does it all come from?
A lifetime of accumulation
eventually becomes a burden.
Family treasures, garage sale bargains
too good to discard,
mementos from a friend's sale,
keepsakes from the past;
all too precious to let go
because
"I might need that sometime."

Things
define us, burden us,
make our lives easier
and harder.
Our needs and our wants
are often at odds.

Perhaps
"getting home before dark"
includes the grace and the freedom
to share and give away,
turn loose and release
the abundance
of our
STUFF.

Contest Sponsor

Greencroft Communities strives to be more than whatever image comes to mind when you hear the words "retirement community." Not a nursing home. Not a place where old people sit around and do jigsaw puzzles or needlework. Not where seniors blankly stare out the window as the rest of the world rushes by. Our communities are vibrant homes and workplaces — places where people live and where people work. They offer a continuum of care, from independent living and at-home services to assisted living and skilled nursing care. They offer a wide range of stimulating activities and creative opportunities—classes, concerts, gardening, quilting, woodworking, fitness, art, singing in a choir or playing in an orchestra, and other hobbies.

They also provide work opportunities, for activities staff, therapists, nurses, aides, social workers, chaplains and other caretakers and staff. Many of these people are at their community because they care and they feel a call. Our CROFT Values — Creativity, Respect, Openness, Fairness and Teamwork — both guide and reflect how team members relate to residents and to each other.

Greencroft Communities is a regional organization that currently includes six affiliate communities in Indiana and Ohio. It also has management contracts with several additional communities in Illinois and Ohio. Each community is a no-for-profit entity with its own local Board of Directors appointed by the Greencroft Communities Board of Directors. MHS Alliance, an agency of the Mennonite Church, appoints the board for Greencroft Communities and provides a connection with the church. Some of our communities are from other denominational groups. Our residents come from over 20 faith traditions.

Approximately 2,000 residents call these communities "home." We invite you to visit and consider them as a possibility for your own encore years.

- **Walnut Hills**, Walnut Creek, Ohio, opened in 1971 and serves 270 residents
- **Southfield Village**, South Bend, Indiana, opened in 2000 and serves 130 residents
- **Oak Grove Christian Retirement Village**, in DeMotte, Indiana, began in 1999 and serves 90 residents
- **Hamilton Grove**, New Carlisle, Indiana, was founded in 1922 and has 275 residents
- **Greencroft Middlebury**, Middlebury, Indiana, opened in 2004 and serves 45 residents
- **Greencroft Goshen**, Goshen, Indiana, began in 1967 and serves 1,100 residents

Please also visit us online at www.greencroft.org

GREENCROFT COMMUNITIES